RIVIERA

RIVIERA

RECIPES FROM THE COAST OF FRANCE AND ITALY

MÉLANIE MASARIN

WILLIAM MORROW

An Imprint of HarperCollins*Publishers*

To my grandmother Mymo,
who used to live by the sea and
now lives with the stars.
Thank you for teaching me
that cooking comes from the heart.

CONTENTS

INTRODUCTION

A beaming grandmother and her first and
arguably favorite grandchild (me).

My grandmother started this kitchen cookbook
at the age of eighteen and used it every
day until her last. It is my most prized
possession.

Hi, I'm Mélanie. I moved to the United States when I was seventeen, and food has since been my way back home to my French Italian family now spread between Paris and the south of France. In New York, my tiny apartment always had more guests than chairs at dinner parties—gathering people around a table was my way of recreating the warmth of home. And it's partially what inspired me to create Ghia, nonalcoholic aperitifs inspired by the Italian amari of the Riviera and the flavors of my childhood.

I always get asked what food pairs well with Ghia and the answer is simple: the food that inspired it. Food that requires no fancy ingredients and leaves no waste behind—cucina povera.

I always thought I would write a cookbook "someday," in that mythical future when life slows down enough to write about it. But here I am, sharing these recipes now because they feel more relevant than ever: handmade pasta for neighbors, instructions whispered over the phone on how to carve a chicken, unfussy dishes that bring Mediterranean warmth to kitchens everywhere. These aren't recipes that require you to marinate and stew all day. They're designed to bring flavor to every bite and slow down our fast-paced lives ever so slightly. A one-way ticket from New York to Nice, designed for limited pots, pans, and patience.

And no, I'm not a chef—that's the point. My "Mediterranean cuisine" is my garlic- and olive-oil-scented melting pot of recipes, my delicious excuses to bring people together. These are the recipes I grew up on—fun and versatile dishes that stretch a limited pantry. With few ingredients, rarely more than ten, I want to transport you to the coastal tables of my childhood. Ratatouille, branzino, or stuffed vegetables—these recipes can last a few meals and are meant to be shared with the people you love.

This is a collection for people who want to host without stress, who have no professional training or kitchen but want to feel the joy of bringing people together around a table. If I'm successful, this book will make the food secondary—only a catalyst for moments of connection. It won't teach you how to make elaborate pastries—I would have to figure that out first—but it will open your eyes to the twelve different things you can do with a single lemon and help you make the most of your market haul without fearing that you're missing an ingredient. At its heart, this is a book about hospitality and thoughtfulness and an ode to summer—from the dishes I make ahead so I can be present to greet my friends to the biscotti that will sit on their espresso saucer, an excuse to make the conversation last a while longer. Excellent cooking, I was taught by my grandmother, comes from the heart.

THE HEAD CHEF: MYMO

My grandmother Mymo lived frugally yet taught me how to make every table feel generous and abundant. Her kitchen on the Riviera, where I spent every summer, was a crossroads of flavors from everywhere she had lived—from Lyon, where I was born, to the northern coast of Italy, where she would often escape. She was determined, one could even say stubborn, a trait I inherited along with many others. She taught herself English and Italian, which she spoke better than my dad's Venetian family. She was endlessly curious and inventive. The only thing I have ever known her not to know how to do was whistle, but it never mattered—she made her own happy humming noise when lost in her kitchen, her fingers fragrant with fresh garlic as she scribbled in her kitchen notebook.

I was happy being the petit sous-chef, and most days I would get to use the fun mill to make her pomodoro. If my parents weren't around, I was allowed to have a full bowl of it as my main course with nothing else to ruin its perfect taste. She understood that there could never be too much of a good thing—pomodoro for me, cooking with her eldest grandchild for her.

When she passed away almost ten years ago, she left me the handwritten cookbook she started when she was eighteen. It is my most prized possession, full of the rules I also live by:

- The market decides the menu.
- Make unfussy food people will want to eat.
- Follow recipes loosely and adapt them a lot.
- Share food generously.
- Credit recipes borrowed from friends.

Mymo had a saying, *Il n'y a que des bonnes choses dedans*—"There are only good things in it"—which really means "If there are only good things in it, it will taste good." I catch myself using it a lot when improvising in the kitchen, though I can attest firsthand that this last statement does not always hold true.

A COAST OF CONVERGENCE

The Riviera exists in between. Between France and Italy, between mountains and sea, between tradition and pleasure. This thin strip of coastline has always been a place of convergence, where influences collide and merge into something entirely its own.

This is where France relaxes into Italy, where the formality of French cuisine softens under the Mediterranean sun. The flavors don't recognize borders—Italian dialects mix with Provençal in the streets, and pissaladière sits next to pizza, pasta with pistou alongside bouillabaisse. The place has always welcomed outsiders while maintaining its own distinct identity, where local fishermen dock their boats next to luxury yachts, and both find the perfect bowl of soupe de poisson at the port.

Step off the TGV at Avignon station in summer and Provence greets you before you've even left the platform—local farmers set up their stands right there in the station hall, their morning's harvest still warm from the fields. I always pause to fill a crate before heading to my parents' home in Eygalières: tomatoes that smell like sunshine, apricots so ripe they barely make the journey, a jar of olive oil from trees I can see from their terrace. "If Provence is the store, the Riviera is the display window," Roger Vergé once said. The proud artisans of Provence—the olive oil pressers, the cheese makers, the shepherds raising prized Sisteron lamb—create the foundation for everything that makes the Riviera's cuisine what it is. Their carefully crafted ingredients journey from these lavender-scented valleys to find their place on plates served with a view of the Mediterranean.

A MEDITERRANEAN "DIET"

Growing up, I learned that the best "diet" isn't really a diet at all and that food, above all, is for eating and being happy. Mediterranean cuisine is simple: It's built around good olive oil, seasonal vegetables, and whole ingredients, so it naturally reduces inflammation without ever feeling restrictive. As such, I never heard my parents demonize a single ingredient. Each had its purpose and place, in moderation. Pasta was good to keep me full for long days at the barre practicing ballet, and dessert was just meant to be delicious and enjoyed. At my family's table, I learned that health flows naturally from good ingredients, careful preparation, and meals shared in good company. It's also what these recipes aim to share.

FOOD PHILOSOPHY

I learned early on that the market makes the menu. The season's first apricots are special, and they deserve to be the special.

Just like my mom and grandmother waited for the lemons to ripen before making limoncello, I've learned to anticipate what each season has to offer. I believe in the power of a home-cooked meal above all else, and it's much easier to get cooking when you have ingredients that make you excited.

Whenever possible, I try to support local farmers who follow organic practices—every purchase from them is a vote for the kind of food system we want to sustain. Their carrots

might be knobbier, but they taste like actual carrots—the kind that remind you why you love vegetables in the first place. When I spend a bit more on good seasonal produce, I think of it as an investment in flavor and in the people who grow our food with care. Making meals at home, even simple ones, lets you appreciate these ingredients fully.

I would lie if I said I didn't wish I could have rhubarb year-round, so like most French people, my freezer is always full, as I try to stretch the warm seasons just a little longer.

These recipes are meant to be adapted, wherever your ingredients come from. I understand that farmers' markets aren't available to everyone, and the same goods aren't available year-round, and that's okay.

The beauty of these dishes is that they stem more from core principles than strict rules and will likely work with what you have. I just want to get you cooking, and trust me, the rest will follow.

A WELL-STOCKED PANTRY

A thoughtful pantry means you're always halfway to dinner. The ingredients I keep on hand aren't many, but they're carefully chosen. Mediterranean cooking proves how far a modest pantry can take you, conjuring up summer flavors any time of year.

SALT: This might be the most important ingredient in your kitchen. I keep two kinds: Diamond Crystal kosher salt for cooking (which

is what all measurements in this book use—I prefer it because the crystals dissolve easily and stick to food better. If you're using Morton's, use about half the amount) and what I call "surface salts," flaky salts like Maldon for finishing. The difference isn't just about timing—these flaky surface salts add texture and create little bursts of salinity that transform each bite.

OLIVE OIL: In Mediterranean cooking, olive oil isn't just a cooking medium—it's a core ingredient. Many dishes in this book are generously bathed in it, which might seem extravagant until you realize that this oil can often be strained and reused. The quality of your olive oil will make or break a dish, so I keep two types: a good everyday extra virgin olive oil for cooking and a special cold-pressed French or Italian one for finishing. A finishing oil is a little luxury that shines best when drizzled on completed dishes to add aromatic depth and richness. When a recipe calls for frying or requires a neutral oil, I reach for avocado oil—it's my favorite alternative to seed oils, with a high smoke point and clean flavor.

VINEGARS: I'll admit to not being a huge fan of balsamic vinegar in dressings. I often find it too sweet, though I'll never turn down good, aged balsamic with chunks of Parmesan. Instead, my vinegar collection leans toward bright, complex, sometimes good-enough-to-drink vinegars such as red wine or champagne vinegar. The entire line from Tart is a staple in my kitchen—their Oro Blanco and citrus vinegars transform a simple salad dressing, and a splash in sparkling water makes a perfect afternoon refresher.

ANCHOVIES AND ANCHOVY SAUCE: A splash of anchovy sauce or a few fillets melted into your base adds an unexpected depth that will elevate your cooking to restaurant-level complexity. You'll find them in surprising places throughout this book—even in meat dishes.

HERBS, THE HEART OF COOKING

In the south of France and throughout northern Italy, herbs aren't garnish—they're the heart of any dish. Basil grows abundantly and rosemary is almost invasive, spreading in wild bushes. While fresh herbs are my preference, don't dismiss dried ones; they both have their place and dried herbs are better than none. In this book, herbs are often interchangeable—what matters is using them generously. Here are some of my favorites:

BASIL: The quintessential Mediterranean herb, used as an ingredient rather than a garnish. Best fresh and before it flowers, it's a tomato's eternal companion. You'll find it layered whole in my Green Lasagna (page 115) and blended into Pistou (page 94). It's what distinguishes a Mediterranean green sauce from a South American chimichurri.

PARSLEY: In Europe, we often use curly parsley, and never just a sprinkle. It's the base of my favorite green sauce and persillade, traditionally famous with escargot but equally delicious with vegetables and seafood. When paired with garlic and butter, often it becomes the foundation of a dish.

THYME AND ROSEMARY: These sturdy herbs infuse broths and oils beautifully. While too tough to eat, they leave their essence behind. I particularly love fried rosemary as a crispy topping on Panisse (page 27) or fries.

CHERVIL: Less common in America but beloved in France, where we treat it as a delicate lettuce leaf in its own right. It's often paired with other tender greens, like mâche, in the French tradition of fragrant salads. If you see it, buy it!

DILL: The classic companion to fish, dill is quite polarizing, like anise and fennel. If it's not your taste, mint makes a good substitute. I love it with goat cheese or crème fraîche, salmon, or anything lemony. It should be eaten fresh and makes a wonderful addition to green salads or feta dressing.

SAVORY: My favorite herb for chicken—it's a sleeper hit. It adds an unexpected depth to broths and meats, which I've come to crave.

MINT: The first summer salads with mint signal the season's change. Different varieties offer subtle variations in freshness. Beautiful with fruit, in drinks, or scattered over fresh strawberries. Mint is for more than just tea!

BAY LEAVES: Fresh or dried, they're a quiet hero in the kitchen. They work their subtle magic in almost every broth, sauce, and stew in this book. I add them to cooking beans or lentils and tuck them into braises.

SAGE: More common in Italian cooking than French, its velvety leaves are particularly wonderful fried with butter and pasta.

MARJORAM: Slightly spicy with a gentle kick, it seeps beautifully into butter sauces and adds an unexpected savor to cheese dishes. Marjoram works wonderfully both fresh and dried, with distinctly different profiles. A natural match for chicken and grilled meats, it's the most floral herb I use besides lavender.

PANTRY

Lunch at Tuba Club in Marseille.

My dad, siblings, and I wore our best fashion for a day trip to Monaco.

GARLIC CONFIT

MAKES ABOUT 2 CUPS (450 G) • **PREP TIME:** 15 MINUTES • **COOK TIME:** 1 HOUR

To confit is to cook for a long time as a method of preservation—it softens and sweetens the texture and taste of garlic to an almost buttery, spreadable paste. Garlic confit is perfect for people who don't like the strong taste of raw garlic, and it's a great base for a tartine or as an addition to your vinaigrettes.

5 garlic heads (50 to 60 cloves) (I use whole heads with the bottoms cut, but you can choose to peel them)

3 rosemary or thyme sprigs

1¾ teaspoons kosher salt

15 whole black peppercorns

2 to 3 cups olive oil, or enough to fully submerge

1. In a large saucepan, combine the garlic, herbs, salt, and peppercorns. Add the olive oil to submerge and heat over low heat for 1 hour. The oil should simmer slightly but not boil. The cooking time may vary depending on the size of the garlic cloves; the larger ones will take longer to cook. The garlic is ready when it is soft and can escape out of its skin with the back of a fork.

2. Let cool, then pour the cloves and oil into a jar, cover, and store in the refrigerator. Make sure that all the garlic is covered with oil. Use a clean spoon each time you want to collect the cloves or the fragrant oil, which can be saved and used for cooking. The confit will keep in the refrigerator for 3 months. The oil may solidify when chilled—this is normal. Let it come to room temperature before using.

MAKE IT YOUR OWN

Play with the aromatics: bay leaves, red pepper flakes, or citrus peel can add different dimensions of flavor. For a sweeter result, try adding a tablespoon of honey.

GIARDINIERA

MAKES ABOUT 2 QUARTS • **PREP TIME:** 30 MINUTES • **PICKLING TIME:** 4 TO 5 DAYS IN THE REFRIGERATOR

Giardiniera ("gardener") is a version of Italian pickles, sometimes chopped into a rough relish and used as a sauce. It's common as a pre-meal snack, or aperitivo, and that's how I prefer to consume it—I find that the vinegar greatly helps with digestion before a heavier meal. I love to use radishes and cauliflower because they look beautiful, but truly any fresh vegetable will work. Experiment with herbs and spices too: coriander, mustard seed, red pepper flakes, and dill are classic, but if I have marjoram, savory, or juniper berries, I love to throw those in.

FOR THE PICKLES

½ **cauliflower head**

2 **carrots**

2 **celery stalks**

1 **red bell pepper**

1 **spicy pepper (I like serrano or jalapeño; optional)**

Handful of radishes

Herbs (I love dill or marjoram)

FOR THE DRESSING

2 **cups (480 ml) light vinegar, such as apple cider vinegar, white vinegar, white wine vinegar, or champagne vinegar**

2 **cups (480 ml) olive oil**

2 **teaspoons kosher salt**

1 **teaspoon freshly ground black pepper**

3 **teaspoons mixed spices (I like oregano, red pepper flakes, and mustard seeds)**

1. PREPARE THE VEGETABLES: Wash the vegetables and herbs. Trim, peel, and seed them as desired, then cut them into pieces no larger than 2 inches. If you plan on using your giardiniera as a condiment, smaller pieces are best. I like to serve mine at the beginning of the meal, so I prefer more substantial pieces.

2. MAKE THE DRESSING: In a large bowl, combine the dressing ingredients with 2 cups (480 ml) water.

3. PICKLE THE VEGETABLES: Pack the vegetables in two 32-ounce pickling jars with a lid and pour the dressing over them to submerge all the vegetables. Seal the jar.

4. Refrigerate for at least 4 days—the more patient you are, the more flavorful it will get. A refrigerated unopened jar of pickles will keep for up to 1 year. Use within 3 months if opened.

HOMEMADE BROTHS

SERVES 4 TO 6 • **PREP TIME:** 15 MINUTES • **COOK TIME:** 2 HOURS FOR VEGETABLE BROTH; 6 TO 10 HOURS FOR MEAT BROTH

A homemade broth turns this week's scraps into next week's delight. By concentrating flavor and nutrients and turning them into delicious pockets of juices, the broth can become the base of an easy soup or the key ingredient to making your braise and pasta taste restaurant level.

Olive oil

Vegetable scraps, such as onion ends and skins, garlic skins, carrot peelings, celery butts

Aromatics, such as whole black peppercorns, herb fronds and leaves, Parmesan rinds, ginger slices, citrus peels, soy sauce or miso

Meat and bones, such as cooked beef, lamb, or pork bones; cooked or raw chicken bones, wing tips, and necks; fish bones, heads, and tails

Kosher salt

1. Keep vegetable scraps, bones, and Parmesan rinds in a freezer bag in the freezer until you have enough to make a bouillon: vegetable scraps add sweetness, bones provide richness, and aromatics bring depth. Just avoid tough stems, which can make your broth bitter.

2. In a large stockpot with a splash of olive oil, sear the alliums and aromatics over medium heat until golden brown, about 4 minutes. This is an optional step, but color is flavor that will add depth and nuttiness to your broth.

3. Add the rest of your vegetable and meat and bones ingredients along with enough water to cover them and turn the heat to high. Leave the pot uncovered—you want the water to evaporate so the flavors in your broth can concentrate. As soon as the water starts to boil, reduce the heat to a gentle simmer and cook for as long as needed; meat broths will take at least 6 hours or overnight until all the collagen and flavor has been infused into the water. Vegetarian broths should be ready in a couple of hours. Taste along the way and add salt as needed.

4. Skim the frothy clusters off the top and strain loosely, no need to worry about every tiny particle. Let the broth cool to room temperature, then portion into ice cube molds or storage containers and refrigerate or freeze until ready to use. For meat broths, you can choose to remove some of the fat at the top when it cools; I like to keep it refrigerated in a separate jar to cook with.

5. These broths will keep in the refrigerator for up to 4 days or in the freezer for 6 months.

CHERRY TOMATO CONFIT

MAKES ABOUT 2 CUPS (480 ML) • **PREP TIME:** 15 MINUTES • **COOK TIME:** 4 HOURS

Confit cherry tomatoes are my adult version of candy. They burst into delightfully sweet and intense juices—my favorite condiment to add to any chicken, pasta, or toast, but I can also never resist them by the spoonful. They're a great substitute for tomato paste if you don't have it on hand. Each September, I beg the farmers at the market for trays of their last, softer tomatoes to take home and confit, hoping they'll last me through the winter, which they never do.

1 pound (450 g) cherry tomatoes

3 thyme or rosemary sprigs or a couple bay leaves

1 garlic head, separated into cloves and peeled (10 to 12 cloves)

½ cup (120 ml) olive oil if you plan on eating them right away, plus 1 cup (240 ml) olive oil to submerge the tomatoes if preserving

Kosher salt and freshly ground black pepper

1. Preheat the oven to 225°F.

2. Spread the tomatoes, herbs, and garlic in a single layer on a sheet pan or in a large oven-safe skillet. Drizzle with the ½ cup olive oil, then sprinkle with salt and pepper.

3. Slow-roast for 4 hours, or until the tomatoes are wrinkled, with the skin tearing. You can go faster by turning up the heat a little, but the slow-cooking process helps sweeten the juices significantly.

4. When the tomatoes are cool enough to handle, taste them for salt. Strip the leaves from the herbs and add the herbs back to the tomatoes. Keep the garlic cloves intact (see Note). Transfer the ingredients of the pan to an airtight container and refrigerate for up to 5 days. If you want to refrigerate the tomatoes for longer or freeze them, add the remaining 1 cup oil, leaving an inch at the top of the jar as the oil will congeal when cold. Stored this way they will keep for about 1 week in the refrigerator or up to 6 months in the freezer.

> **NOTE:** *I like to keep the garlic cloves whole and decide what to do with them when I'm ready to use my tomatoes. If I'm making toast, for instance, I'll spread the garlic first, then add tomatoes on top. If I'm dropping tomatoes into a soup as garnish, I'll omit the garlic.*

CURED LEMONS

MAKES ONE 16-OUNCE (500 ML) JAR • **PREP TIME:** 30 MINUTES
CURING TIME: 4 TO 6 WEEKS AT ROOM TEMPERATURE

Once a year, my grandmother's friend would invite her over to pick as many lemons from her trees as she could fit in her car. For days afterward, she and my mom would zest and peel and squeeze them into large batches of limoncello that they would enjoy during late nights the following summer. My job then was to observe and cut some of the lemons to cure them in salt, transforming their sharp acidity into a mellow, complex flavor so delicious with meats and rice. Thirty years later and 6,000 miles away, I still hold to this tradition of curing lemons collected on trees whenever I see them. The juice of cured lemons is also my favorite natural sweetener for Ghia cocktails.

¾ cup (180 g) kosher salt

3 or 4 large organic lemons, cut into eighths or quarters

1. Cover the bottom of a 16-ounce mason jar with 2 tablespoons of salt, then place a layer of lemons on top. Keep layering the salt and lemons until you reach the top of the jar. End with salt on top, packing everything tightly so that the whole jar of lemons is soaked in salty lemon juice.

2. Seal the jar and let it sit at room temperature for 4 to 6 weeks. The lemons are fully cured once they swim in clear sweet and sour juices. They will keep at room temperature for up to 6 months.

> **NOTE:** *Cured lemons are great for stuffing a chicken, small-diced and used in a gremolata, in a salad dressing, or wherever some subtle citrus is needed.*

CURED EGG YOLKS

MAKES 4 CURED YOLKS • **PREP TIME:** 15 MINUTES • **CURING TIME:** 7 DAYS IN THE REFRIGERATOR

While the recipe for cured egg yolks doesn't come straight out of the Riviera, the principle of *cucina povera*, not wasting so much as a bread crumb, was the first rule I learned in the kitchen. Many meringues and pavlovas and chocolate mousses mean lonely egg yolks—and curing them is the most delicious way to make sure they don't go to waste. Cured for 7 days in salt and sugar, they become savory, umami gems with a cheese-like texture. Shower them as garnish on salads, pasta, or soups—anywhere you'd reach for aged cheese like Parmesan.

1 cup (240 g) kosher salt
½ cup (100 g) sugar
4 large egg yolks

1. Combine the salt and sugar and spread half of it in a storage container that's wide enough to fit all four yolks about 1 inch apart. Using the back of a spoon, make 4 shallow indents in the salt mixture, then carefully lay each yolk in its little nest. Sprinkle the remaining salt and the sugar mixture on top to cover the yolks fully.

2. Seal the container and refrigerate for 7 days.

3. After 7 days, the salt will have pulled most of the moisture from the yolks. Rinse the yolks briefly under cold water to remove the excess salt.

4. Shave the yolks on top of toast, pasta, sandwiches, or anywhere else you'd use cheese. They keep in an airtight container in the refrigerator for up to 4 weeks.

PÂTE BRISÉE

MAKES TWO 12-INCH CRUSTS • **PREP TIME:** 15 MINUTES • **REST TIME:** 1 HOUR OR OVERNIGHT

Pâte brisée, which literally means "broken pastry" for its delicate, flaky texture, is a piecrust we can buy for a few euros in any French supermarket, and I've gotten used to having them handy: They make the base of any quiche or tart for a last-minute gathering. But nothing beats the taste of this homemade all-butter version. While doughs are generally daunting to make by hand, this one takes just a couple minutes in a food processor. The only rule is to use very cold butter and ice water (water swirled with a lot of ice), and don't forget to make extra for your freezer.

2½ cups (300 g) all-purpose flour, plus more for the work surface

2 teaspoons kosher salt

2 sticks (225 g) cold unsalted butter, cut into cubes

½ cup (120 ml) ice water

> **NOTE:** *If using for a dessert, you can use 1 teaspoon sugar and ½ teaspoon salt, but I almost always just use the savory version I have on hand for my sweet desserts, as I find a touch of salt complements fruits so nicely.*

1. If using a food processor, place the flour and salt in the bowl and pulse to combine. Add the cold butter cubes and pulse until the mixture resembles coarse sand, with some pea-size pieces of butter still visible. With the motor running, slowly drizzle in the ice water just until the dough starts coming together. Stop before it forms a ball, if you pinch some dough, it should hold together. If working by hand, grate very cold butter on the large holes of a box grater, then quickly transfer it to a bowl with the flour and salt and mix in the butter with your fingertips until crumbly. Add the ice water and gather into a dough.

2. Lightly flour your work surface, then turn out the dough and divide it in half. Shape each piece into a disk, wrap well, and refrigerate for at least 1 hour.

3. When ready to use, let the dough soften slightly at room temperature, about 10 minutes. On a floured surface, roll into a 12-inch round, about ⅛ inch thick, or slightly larger than the pie dish you're using. If the dough feels too soft at any point, slide it onto a baking sheet and refrigerate for 10 minutes.

4. To store, place the rolled dough between sheets of parchment paper, fold into quarters, and freeze for up to 3 months. Let frozen dough thaw overnight in the refrigerator before using.

PÂTE FEUILLETÉE

ALL-BUTTER PUFF PASTRY

MAKES TWO 12 × 16-INCH SHEETS • **PREP TIME:** 30 MINUTES • **REST TIME:** 2 HOURS+

I avoided making puff pastry for years; it felt like one of those things best left to professionals. Once I tried it, I realized that it's actually quite forgiving and meditative—rolling, folding, chilling. Keeping everything as cold as possible is essential, as it's those cold flakes of butter that create magically crispy layers when they hit the hot oven. Nothing compares to a tarte tatin (see page 46) or Pissaladière (page 32) made on a homemade puff pastry.

2½ cups (300 g) plus 2 tablespoons all-purpose flour, plus more for the work surface

2 teaspoons kosher salt

⅔ cup (160 ml) ice water

2½ sticks (280 g) cold unsalted butter

1. In a food processor, pulse the 2½ cups of flour and salt to combine. With the motor running, slowly add the ice water until the dough just comes together. Lightly flour your work surface, then turn out the dough and knead it briefly until smooth. Shape the dough into a square, wrap well, and refrigerate to keep it cool—the colder your ingredients, the flakier your pastry.

2. Let the butter soften just enough to be workable: it should be cold but able to bend without breaking. In a medium bowl, mix the butter with the remaining 2 tablespoons flour. Press the butter mixture into a 6-inch square between two pieces of parchment. Refrigerate until firm but not rock-hard, about 30 minutes.

3. On a floured surface, roll the chilled dough into a rectangle twice the size of the butter square. Place the cold butter in the center and fold the sides of the dough over it like an envelope, making sure the butter is completely sealed inside. This is the first turn.

4. Roll this package into a long rectangle about 18 × 6 inches and about ¼ inch thick. Fold each end of the rectangle over the center into thirds, like a letter. This is the second turn. If the butter feels soft or starts to stick, wrap and chill for 30 minutes.

5. Repeat this rolling and folding two more times for a total of four turns. Do not worry if your folds aren't perfect—as long as you keep everything cold, the pastry will still puff up in the oven.

6. After the final turn, wrap the dough well and refrigerate it for at least 2 hours or overnight.

7. When ready to use, cut the dough in half and roll each piece into a 12 × 16-inch rectangle. Use as directed or fold between parchment paper and freeze for up to 3 months.

APERITIVO

The magnificent Hotel du Couvent in Nice, in a
restored convent atop the old city. They kindly
welcomed us for part of the shoot.

A Spritz a day keeps the doctor away.

RADISHES WITH BUTTER

SERVES 4 TO 6 • **PREP TIME:** 15 MINUTES + CHILLING

Every American friend of mine who visits Paris for the first time brings back tales of radishes with butter. For good reason—they're the simplest combination and also the most delightful. When I was growing up, my father would steer us to the dining table with radishes carved into boats or flowers—tiny sculptures full of nooks and crannies whose sole purpose was to cloak soft pockets of butter.

1 stick (113 g) unsalted butter
1 bunch radishes (about 24)
Flaky salt, for serving

1. Trim the radishes and leave them in the refrigerator until you're ready to dip them in butter.

2. Place the butter in a small microwave-safe bowl and microwave for about 20 seconds, until it's just about half melted. With a fork or small whisk, stir the butter so it's silky and uniform.

3. Dip the radishes halfway into the butter and place them carefully on a sheet pan. Refrigerate until you're ready to serve them, then accompany with a small bowl of nice flaky salt.

RADISH TOAST

This toast is so straightforward yet feels so luxurious: the crisp snap of thinly sliced radishes against rich, creamy butter create layers of texture I find irresistible. Add a pinch of flaky salt on top, and this is a perfect bite to me. I don't know if this is officially a Riviera recipe, but it's something I have so often at home that I just assume it's a local tradition.

1 slice country bread

2 tablespoons cold unsalted butter

2 medium radishes

Flaky salt to taste

Grill the bread in a toaster or on a pan in the oven until crisp. Spread a thin layer of the butter on the toast. With a knife or a mandoline, slice the radishes very thinly and arrange them on top of the butter, then sprinkle with some flaky salt.

OLIVE AND HAM SAVORY "CAKE"

SERVES 8 TO 10 • **PREP TIME:** 20 MINUTES • **COOK TIME:** 40 TO 45 MINUTES

A French "cake" pronounced the American way means a savory cake: quite eggy and fluffy, part cake and part soufflé. It's delicious as an appetizer on an *aperitivo* table, but I also love it the next day, sliced and served on a bed of greens. The base of this cake is simple: just one bowl with a base of olive oil and eggs that can also welcome all your leftover chorizo, greens, and even hazelnuts.

⅔ cup (160 ml) olive oil, plus more for greasing

1½ cups (180 g) all-purpose flour

2 teaspoons baking powder

1 teaspoon kosher salt

½ teaspoon freshly ground black pepper

½ cup (120 ml) whole milk

4 large eggs, at room temperature

1 cup (100 g) shredded Gruyère

1 cup (160 g) ¼-inch-diced ham

½ cup pitted green olives

1 cup lightly packed flat-leaf parsley leaves, finely chopped

1. Preheat the oven to 400°F. Grease a 9 × 5-inch loaf pan or cake tin with some olive oil, then line it with parchment paper, leaving some overhang on the long sides for easier removal of the cake.

2. In a large bowl, whisk together the flour, baking powder, salt, and pepper. Add the olive oil, milk, and eggs and whisk to form a smooth batter. Add the Gruyère (reserving 2 tablespoons), ham, olives, and parsley and stir to incorporate.

3. Scrape the batter into the prepared pan and smooth the top. Sprinkle with the reserved 2 tablespoons cheese. Bake for 40 to 45 minutes, until golden brown on top and the tip of a knife inserted into the center comes out clean.

4. Transfer the pan to a wire rack and let cool for 10 minutes. Unmold the cake and slice to serve.

5. Refrigerate the leftover cake in an airtight container for up to 2 days.

PANISSE

SERVES 4 TO 6 (ABOUT 24 PIECES) • **PREP TIME:** 20 MINUTES • **COOK TIME:** 25 MINUTES
PLUS AT LEAST 2 HOURS CHILLING

Panisse are really just chickpea fries, which sounds fancy but isn't! They're shatteringly crisp on the outside, with creamy and springy middles. The easy-to-make batter sets into a wobbly mass that you'll slice into batons. In Provence, they are fried in olive oil, but you are welcome to use a neutral oil like avocado oil. This recipe is very easy to scale up or down. Make more than you think you need—they have a way of vanishing the moment they hit the table, still warm and singing with salt.

½ cup (120 ml) olive oil or neutral oil, for frying, plus more for greasing

1 cup (120 g) chickpea flour

2 sage or rosemary sprigs

1 teaspoon kosher salt

6 tablespoons unsalted butter

Flaky salt, for finishing

1. Grease a quarter sheet pan or 8-inch square baking pan with olive oil.

2. In a medium saucepan over medium heat, whisk together the chickpea flour and kosher salt with 1½ cups (350 ml) water until smooth. Add the butter and stir constantly until the mixture is like thick hummus and pulls away from the sides of the pan, 10 to 15 minutes. Panisse is hard to overmix and will break easily if not mixed enough, so don't be precious with it.

3. Pour the batter into the prepared pan and smooth the top. Refrigerate for at least 2 hours or until fully set. Unmold the cooled panisse slab onto a cutting board and cut it into rough

batons about 6 inches long, or as long as they can hold their shape without breaking.

4. In a large skillet, heat up a knuckle's worth (about ½ inch) of olive oil over medium heat. Add the rosemary sprigs to the oil, then, working in batches, add the panisse batons. Cook them evenly on all sides until crisp and golden brown all over, 1 to 2 minutes per side, up to 8 minutes total. Add more oil as needed between batches.

5. Transfer the panisse and sage sprigs to paper towels or a cooling rack and sprinkle liberally with flaky salt. Crush the fried rosemary leaves between your fingers to top the batons.

6. Serve hot—they look nice in paper cones, like street vendors do in Nice.

> **NOTE:** *Traditional panisse is deep-fried for efficiency's sake, but whenever I come across a recipe for deep-frying, I try to adapt it to shallow frying, which works great with this recipe.*

ANCHOIADE AND CRUDITÉS

SERVES 6 TO 8 • **PREP TIME:** 15 MINUTES

This sauce is a staple in the south of France and has many variations—some with stale bread, some with black olives or capers pounded in, others with a handful of fresh herbs. The base recipe is just anchovies pounded with garlic and olive oil until creamy. All taste equally delicious, but I'm partial to garlic and vinegar to make it special.

8 oil-packed anchovy fillets

3 garlic cloves

2 tablespoons red wine vinegar

½ cup (120 ml) olive oil

Freshly ground black pepper to taste

Crudités such as endive leaves, carrots, cauliflower florets, cherry tomatoes, radishes, fennel, and even crusty bread soldiers

1. Using a mortar and pestle, pound the anchovies and garlic into a paste. A small blender or food processor will absolutely work too. Process until just smooth, stopping to scrape down the sides as needed. Gradually work in the vinegar, then drizzle in the olive oil, stirring constantly until creamy. Season with pepper—no salt! The anchovies bring plenty of brininess from the sea.

2. Pour the anchoiade into a small bowl and serve with crudités arranged on a platter.

SOCCA

MAKES 4 FLATBREADS • **PREP TIME:** 10 MINUTES • **REST TIME:** 2 HOURS
COOK TIME: 24 MINUTES

This is a traditional snack from Nice, a town where French and Italian culture meet for a kiss. A flatbread served on a parchment paper, socca is best eaten from a street vendor while walking the Promenade des Anglais, but everyone still seems to enjoy it thoroughly when I make it in my home kitchen.

2 cups (240 g) fine chickpea flour

½ cup (120 ml) olive oil

3 tablespoons minced rosemary

2 teaspoons kosher salt

Flaky salt and freshly ground black pepper to taste

1. In a large bowl, whisk together the chickpea flour, ¼ cup of the olive oil, 2 tablespoons of the rosemary, the kosher salt, and 2 cups (475 ml) water until well-combined. Cover the bowl and let the batter rest for at least 2 hours at room temperature or up to overnight in the refrigerator.

2. Place a 10-inch oven-safe skillet under the broiler and preheat the broiler to high. Heat the skillet for 10 minutes.

3. Remove the skillet from the broiler and pour in 2 tablespoons of the olive oil, followed by a quarter of the batter (about ¾ cup), swirling to create a thick pancake. Broil until the edges of the socca are crisp and the top has spots of char, about 6 minutes.

4. Slide the socca onto a plate and repeat to make 3 more socca. Scatter the socca with the remaining rosemary and finish with some flaky salt and pepper. Wrap each socca in parchment to serve.

SQUASH BLOSSOM FRITTERS

SERVES 4 • **PREP TIME:** 10 MINUTES • **COOK TIME:** 10 MINUTES

I eagerly await squash blossoms at the market—those delicate orange flowers that remind me of my childhood summers in Cannes and the abundant Marché de Forville, where street vendors fry them to order. Here's my homemade version—shallow-fried in avocado oil instead of deep-fried, making them far less daunting to prepare. I use a mix of flours: all-purpose flour for structure and rice flour for extra crispiness.

12 to 16 squash blossoms
½ cup (60 g) all-purpose flour
¼ cup (30 g) rice flour
¾ cup (180 ml) cold sparkling water
1 egg
Avocado oil or other neutral oil, for frying
Flaky salt to taste

1. Have handy a wire rack set in a rimmed sheet pan or line a plate with paper towels. Set aside.

2. Gently open each blossom and remove the stamen. Clean the center gently to remove any extra pollen dust.

3. In a medium bowl, whisk together both flours, the sparkling water, and egg until just combined—a few lumps are fine. The batter will be thin, like heavy cream, but will still coat the blossoms.

4. Heat ½ inch oil in a high-sided skillet over medium-high heat. Gently dip the flowers in the batter one at a time and shake off any excess. Working in batches so as not to crowd the pan, carefully lower them into the hot oil and fry for a couple minutes on each side, until they're golden.

5. Transfer the fritters to the wire rack or prepared plate to drain the excess oil. Sprinkle with flaky salt and serve while hot and crisp.

TARTE SOLEIL

SERVES 8 • **PREP TIME:** 15 MINUTES • **COOK TIME:** 45 MINUTES PLUS 30 MINUTES CHILLING

A tarte soleil is what happens when puff pastry dresses up for a party. While traditionally filled with pesto or tapenade, I've found it works easily with anything that won't run in the oven—from olive paste to pistachio butter. The rays twist outward to create a tear-and-share centerpiece for aperitivo hour. Keep the pastry cold until the last moment—it's the key to those flaky layers.

2 sheets store-bought puff pastry or Pâte Feuilletée (page 15), thawed slightly

1 cup filling of your choice, such as Pistou (page 94), tapenade, tomato sauce, or Anchoiade (page 26)

1 egg, beaten

Flaky salt to taste

1 tablespoon sesame or poppy seeds (optional but pretty)

1. Line a sheet pan with parchment paper. Roll a pastry sheet into a 12-inch round and place it on the prepared sheet pan. Spread the filling evenly on the pastry, leaving a 1-inch border. Brush the border with half of the beaten egg. Roll out a second pastry round and lay it evenly on top of the first. Place a small glass in the center to create the heart of your sun.

2. Preheat the oven to 400°F.

3. Using the glass as a guide, cut the dough like a pizza—first into 4 equal quarters, then divide each quarter into 5 wedges, creating a total of 20 equal wedges. Leave the center intact where the glass sits. Working quickly to keep the dough cool, twist each strip twice. The dough is too warm if it feels soft, stretchy, or sticks to your fingers. If this happens, place the entire sheet pan in the refrigerator for 30 minutes before continuing. Cold dough will give you the most defined, and crispiest, spiral pattern.

4. Brush the top of the pastry with the remaining beaten egg and sprinkle it all over with flaky salt and the seeds (if using). Bake until golden and crisp, 20 to 25 minutes.

5. Serve immediately or within a couple of hours. Do not refrigerate or it will lose its crispiness.

PISSALADIÈRE

SERVES 4 TO 6 • **PREP TIME:** 15 MINUTES • **COOK TIME:** 1 HOUR 15 MINUTES

This is a Provençal tart traditionally made with pizza dough, but I've always preferred to make mine with puff pastry, which creates delightfully crisp layers beneath sweet caramelized onions and briny anchovies. Let the onions slowly collapse and caramelize until they're practically jam—the rest is just assembly.

3 tablespoons olive oil

6 large red onions, halved and thinly sliced

1 teaspoon kosher salt

3 thyme sprigs, leaves stripped

2 teaspoons red wine vinegar

1 teaspoon sugar (optional)

Flaky salt and freshly ground black pepper to taste

12 oil-packed anchovy fillets

½ cup pitted or unpitted Niçoise olives

1 sheet store-bought puff pastry or Pâte Feuilletée (page 15), thawed slightly

1. Preheat the oven to 400°F. Line a sheet pan with parchment paper and set aside.

2. Heat the olive oil in a large skillet over medium-low heat. Add the onions and salt and cook partially covered, stirring occasionally,

until very soft, at least 35 minutes. Increase the heat to medium-high, add the thyme, vinegar, and sugar (if using) and season with flaky salt and pepper. Cook until the onions are deeply caramelized, about another 10 minutes. Let the filling cool completely.

3. Roll out the puff pastry to ⅛-inch thickness and transfer it to the prepared sheet pan. Bake until golden, about 20 minutes.

4. Spread the onion mixture over the pastry, all the way to the edges. Arrange the anchovies on top in a diamond pattern and place one olive in each diamond.

5. Cut into squares and serve warm or at room temperature.

APPETIZERS

A winter walk on La Croisette with my dad and my
grandparents and their dog, Pepsi, 1992.

Metal chairs alongside the Promenade des Anglais.
They're almost the same as the green ones in the
Jardin des Tuileries!

ROASTED RED PEPPERS SOTT'OLIO

MAKES ABOUT 2 CUPS (480 ML) • **PREP TIME:** 45 MINUTES • **COOK TIME:** 10 MINUTES

Here's another pantry staple that never lasts long in my house. While technically the only ingredient needed here is peppers, the other main element is heat. Charring your red peppers on the flame of your stove or grill or under your broiler makes them soft and sweet—somewhere between a vegetable and a condiment. I love to add them to a simple fish or chop them with leftovers as a sandwich filling.

4 red bell or sweet Italian peppers
Your best olive oil, for drizzling
White wine vinegar
Pinch of flaky salt
¼ cup (60 ml) olive oil, for storing

1. Place each pepper over the eye of a gas-burning stove with the flame on high. (Alternatively, line up the peppers side by side on a sheet pan and place on the top rack of the oven, under the broiler set to high.) Cook the peppers, turning them with tongs occasionally, until blistered and blackened all over, about 10 minutes. While still hot, transfer the peppers to a large bowl, cover the bowl with a lid, and let them steam for about 30 minutes, which also helps make peeling them easier.

2. Uncover the bowl and use your clean hands to peel off most of the charred skin from the peppers. Discard the skin, along with the peppers' seeds and stems. Tear the peppers into large strips.

3. To serve, drizzle the peppers with your best olive oil and white wine vinegar, then sprinkle with the flaky salt. Store in an airtight container for a few weeks in the refrigerator or a couple months in the freezer.

GIGANTE BEANS

SERVES 4 TO 6 • **PREP TIME:** 10 MINUTES • **COOK TIME:** 25 MINUTES (IF USING CANNED BEANS) OR 2 HOURS (IF USING DRIED BEANS)

I'll never discourage anyone from using canned beans—they're a staple in my pantry. But there's a particular joy in watching dried beans transform as they slowly simmer, drinking up a garlicky, lemony broth until they're plump and tender. The resulting pot liquor is so good you'll want to have some crusty bread nearby for dipping.

1 pound (450 g) dried gigante beans, soaked overnight

1 yellow onion, halved

6 garlic cloves

½ cup olive oil

2 bay leaves

Zest of 1 lemon

2 tablespoons kosher salt

1 tablespoon black peppercorns

Zest and juice of 1 lemon

Flaky salt to taste

Your best olive oil, for drizzling

1. Drain the soaked beans and place them in a large Dutch oven or other heavy pot with a lid. Cover with water by 2 inches (about 8 cups). Add the onion, garlic, ¼ cup of the olive oil, the bay leaves, half of the lemon zest, the kosher salt, and peppercorns.

2. Bring to a boil, then reduce the heat to a gentle simmer. Partially cover the pot and cook until the beans are creamy and tender, about 1½ hours. Turn off the heat and stir in the lemon juice and the remaining ¼ cup olive oil. Let the beans cool in their liquid—they'll continue to drink up the flavors.

3. Taste the beans for salt and serve them warm with a drizzle of your best olive oil and the remaining lemon zest sprinkled on top.

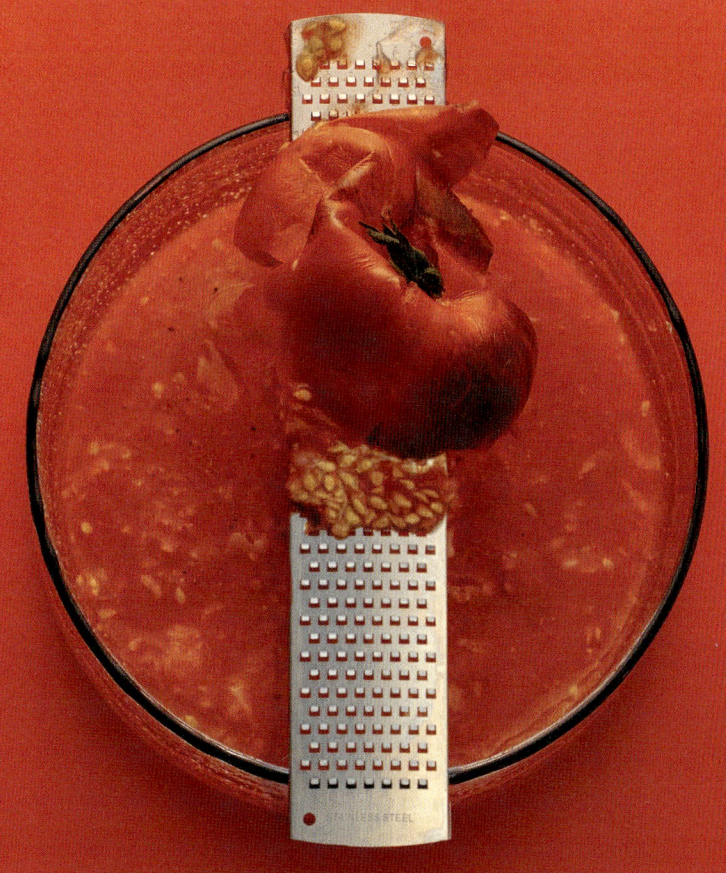

GRATED TOMATO CARPACCIO

SERVES 4 • **PREP TIME:** 10 MINUTES

Inspired by Spain's pan con tomate, for which bread is rubbed with garlic and topped with grated tomato pulp, this dish makes the topping the star of the show. Mix different-colored tomatoes if you can find them; they'll make this simple appetizer look spectacular.

2 pounds (900 g) mixed ripe tomatoes (ideally use different varieties and colors)

2 garlic cloves

3 tablespoons your best olive oil

Flaky salt and freshly ground black pepper to taste

Torn basil leaves, for garnish

1. Working with one color at a time, grate the tomatoes on the coarse side of a box grater directly onto a serving plate in stripes, discarding the skins. Be careful with your fingers! Grate the garlic over the top.

2. Drizzle with the olive oil, season generously with flaky salt and pepper, and top with torn basil leaves.

SALMON CARPACCIO IN OLIVE OIL

SERVES 4 TO 6 • **PREP TIME:** 10 MINUTES

This is my relaxed take on French-style raw fish—it's less precious than a crudo, more forgiving with its slicing (a little density is nice!), and luxurious when bathed in your best olive oil. While I've written this for salmon, use whatever looks best at your local fish market; I've made this with everything from tuna to scallops.

1 pound (450 g) high-quality salmon fillet, pin bones and skin removed

2 tablespoons kosher salt

1 tablespoon pink peppercorns, coarsely crushed

Your best olive oil, for drizzling

Zest and juice of ½ lemon

¼ teaspoon Espelette pepper

1 tablespoon capers, drained

Fresh dill, for garnish

Flaky salt to taste

1. Season the salmon generously on both sides with the salt and crushed pink peppercorns. Wrap it tightly in plastic and let it rest in the refrigerator for at least 4 hours or overnight. Set a serving plate in the refrigerator as well.

2. When you're ready to serve, rinse the salmon quickly and pat it dry. While it's still cold from the refrigerator, cut it into roughly ¼-inch slices, but don't worry—they don't need to be perfect.

3. Arrange the slices in overlapping rows on the cold plate. Drizzle with olive oil and scatter with lemon zest over the top. Just before serving, add a squeeze of lemon juice, the Espelette pepper, capers, and some fresh dill. Finish with some flaky salt.

4. Keep any leftovers in an airtight container covered in olive oil in the refrigerator for up to 3 days or quickly sear the slices in a hot pan for a different meal entirely.

MAKE IT YOUR OWN

FISH: Any high-quality, freshly caught fish, such as fresh sardines, mullet, tuna

HERBS: Bay leaf (refrigerator resting stage); dill, basil, or purslane (as a garnish)

HEAT: Minced jalapeño, grated garlic, minced onion, thinly sliced shallots

GARNISH: Thinly sliced radishes, olives, caper berries

ACID: Lemon, lime, a splash of vinegar of your choice

SALT: ponzu sauce, Cured Lemons (page 10)

SIMPLE CRUDO

SERVES 4 • **PREP TIME:** 15 MINUTES

Don't let raw fish intimidate you—this is one of the simplest ways to serve pristine seafood. The key is buying the freshest fish possible. Ask for a center-cut piece and look for the lines running through the flesh—that's the grain. Slice perpendicular to those lines, like cutting across the stripes of a zebra, for the most tender bites. A sharp knife helps, but perfection isn't the goal; slightly thicker slices are actually lovely here. Scallops work beautifully too.

3 tablespoons olive oil

2 tablespoons capers, drained and patted dry

1 pound (450 g) very fresh white fish, such as sea bream or whatever looks best

1 orange

4 caper berries

Your favorite vinegar (optional, but I love a splash of champagne vinegar)

Your best olive oil

Flaky salt to taste

1. Line a plate with paper towels. Place a serving plate in the refrigerator.

2. In a small saucepan, heat 2 tablespoons of the olive oil over medium heat and fry the capers until crisp, about 1 minute. Drain on the lined plate.

3. Slice the fish thinly against the grain. Arrange the slices in a circle, slightly overlapping, on the chilled serving plate. Using a peeler, create long strips of orange zest. Scatter the fish with the crispy capers, caper berries, and orange zest.

4. Just before serving, squeeze a few drops of orange juice over the fish or, if using, a splash of your favorite vinegar. Drizzle with your best olive oil—it's a core ingredient here—and finish with some flaky salt right before serving.

TOMATO TARTE TATIN

SERVES 4 TO 6 • **PREP TIME:** 15 MINUTES • **COOK TIME:** 35 MINUTES

A classic tatin gets a savory spin here—the fennel and tomatoes collapse into a buttery crust painted with zippy Dijon. While this combination is a favorite of mine in the summer, the method works with any vegetables that caramelize well: onions or shallots in winter; leeks in spring. I love serving this with my "All the Green Things" Shaved Salad (page 68).

All-purpose flour, for the work surface

1 sheet store-bought puff pastry or Pâte Feuilletée (page 15), thawed slightly

1 medium fennel bulb, fronds discarded

2 tablespoons salted butter

2 tablespoons white wine vinegar

1 teaspoon fresh thyme leaves, plus more for serving

1 pint cherry tomatoes, halved lengthwise

1 teaspoon kosher salt

Freshly ground black pepper to taste

1 tablespoon Dijon mustard

½ cup (50 g) freshly finely grated Parmesan or Gruyère

Flaky salt to taste

1. Preheat the oven to 350°F.

2. Lightly flour your work surface, then roll out the pastry into a 12-inch square. Using an overturned 10-inch skillet as a guide, cut out a round of pastry. Chill the pastry in the refrigerator while you prepare the rest of the ingredients.

3. Slice the fennel very thinly (⅛ to ¼ inch). You want it to almost melt with the tomatoes when it cooks.

4. In a 12-inch oven-safe skillet over medium heat, combine the butter, vinegar, and thyme until the butter melts.

5. Lay the fennel slices evenly in the center of the pan and fill the edges and any gaping holes with the halved cherry tomatoes. The vegetables should be snug in the pan. Season with the kosher salt and pepper. Cook on the stove for 5 minutes, until the fennel starts to soften and the juices caramelize.

6. Brush the fennel and tomatoes with the mustard and sprinkle with the cheese. Drape the pastry over the top, tucking the edges down the inner sides of the pan. Cut three slits in the pastry to let any steam escape.

7. Place the skillet in the oven and bake until the pastry dough is deeply golden brown and puffed, 35 to 40 minutes.

8. Let cool for 5 minutes. Run a knife around the edge of the skillet to loosen any stuck bits. Invert a large serving plate over the pan, wrap the plate and pan in a kitchen towel to keep it secure, and quickly flip the tart over. Remove the pan and rearrange any bits that may have come loose on the plate. Scatter the top with thyme and some flaky salt and serve warm or at room temperature.

WINTER VEGETABLE CARPACCIO

SERVES 4 TO 6 • **PREP TIME:** 10 MINUTES

This is my favorite way to use up the unidentifiable vegetables in the bottom of my farm box, especially at the end of winter when I'm eagerly awaiting the first rhubarb and asparagus at the market. A mandoline transforms humble roots into a gorgeous and fun-to-eat appetizer—just be sure to watch your fingers.

1 medium turnip

1 bunch radishes, preferably mixed colors

1 lime (if you can find caviar lime, even better)

Your best olive oil

Flaky salt and freshly ground black pepper to taste

Edible flowers, for garnish (optional)

1. Using the mandoline's thinnest setting, very carefully shave the turnip and radishes into paper-thin slices. Arrange them on a serving plate, overlapping slightly.

2. Zest the lime over the top or, if you have one on hand, sprinkle the pulp of a caviar lime across the plate, then squeeze with lime juice.

3. Drizzle generously with olive oil and season with some flaky salt and pepper. Scatter with edible flowers if you have them.

MOULES GRATINÉES

TOASTED MUSSELS WITH PERSILLADE

SERVES 4 • **PREP TIME:** 15 MINUTES • **COOK TIME:** 10 MINUTES

Moules gratinées are escargots' seaside cousins, topped with persillade, that irresistible mixture of garlic, parsley, butter, and crispy bread crumbs. Homemade bread crumbs make all the difference here, offering a lovely craggy texture.

2 pounds (900 g) fresh mussels (36 to 40 mussels), scrubbed

½ cup (120 ml) dry white wine

5 tablespoons salted butter, softened

3 tablespoons olive oil

4 garlic cloves, finely minced

½ cup (25 g) finely chopped flat-leaf parsley

1 tablespoon kosher salt

½ tablespoon freshly ground black pepper

1 cup (100 g) coarse fresh bread crumbs, made from day-old bread, or panko

1. In a medium Dutch oven or other heavy pot with a lid, cover and steam the mussels in the wine over medium heat until they open, about 3 minutes.

2. Transfer the mussels to a bowl and let them rest until they're cool enough to handle. Discard the cooking liquid and any mussels that haven't opened. Arrange the mussels in their shells open side up on a sheet pan; if any mussels have detached from their shells, give them a home in an empty shell.

3. In a medium bowl, mix the butter, olive oil, garlic, parsley, salt, and pepper until smooth. Top each mussel with a bit of the garlic-herb butter, then sprinkle with a light layer of bread crumbs.

4. Set an oven rack about 5 inches below the broiler and preheat the broiler to high. Broil the mussels, watching carefully, until the bread crumbs are nicely browned, 2 to 3 minutes. Serve immediately.

Moules Gratinées

COQUILLES ST. JACQUES

SEARED SCALLOPS IN THEIR SHELLS

SERVES 4 • **PREP TIME:** 10 MINUTES • **COOK TIME:** 5 MINUTES

Perfect scallops might seem like restaurant territory, but here's the secret: All you need is a very hot pan and good timing. While I love serving them in their shells for presentation, I actually cook them directly in the pan for the best golden crust. A knob of citrus butter melts into a quick pan sauce and a drizzle of chili oil adds just the right amount of heat.

½ stick (60 g) salted butter, softened
1 mandarin or small orange, zested
1 garlic clove, grated on a Microplane
12 sea scallops, preferably in their shells
1 teaspoon kosher salt
¼ cup (60 ml) champagne (optional)
Chili oil, for drizzling
Pinch of flaky salt

1. In a medium bowl, mix the butter, citrus zest, and garlic. Set aside.

2. If the scallops came in shells, slide a thin knife between the shell and meat, cutting the muscle attachments while keeping the white medallion intact for cooking. Keep the shells for serving. Pat the scallops very dry with paper towels—this is crucial for a good sear.

3. Heat a large skillet over high heat until very hot—a drop of water should dance across the surface. Season the scallops with the kosher salt, then sear for 2 minutes, until golden underneath. I like to give them plenty of space in the pan and set them down clockwise, so I know in what order to flip them.

4. Refrain from touching them for a full 2 minutes, so they get a nice crust. Flip and cook the other side for just 15 to 30 seconds. Add the champagne (if using) and let it reduce until syrupy, about 30 seconds. Add a dollop of the citrus butter to the pan, letting it melt into a sauce.

5. Nestle each scallop into a shell and spoon the butter sauce on top. Finish with a drizzle of chili oil and a pinch of flaky salt.

LEEKS IN VINAIGRETTE WITH EGG MIMOSA

SERVES 4 • **PREP TIME:** 20 MINUTES • **COOK TIME:** 25 MINUTES

My grandmother had a trick for getting her grandchildren to eat their vegetables. She'd shower them with fluffy egg mimosa, those golden clouds of crushed hard-boiled egg, which we call "mimosa," like the flower. Here, I've borrowed her method for tender leeks bathed in mustardy vinaigrette.

FOR THE LEEKS AND EGG MIMOSA

8 small (preferably) or 4 large leeks, white and light parts, tops reserved for optional green oil

Kosher salt

3 large eggs

2 tablespoons Dijon mustard

1 tablespoon red wine vinegar

3 tablespoons olive oil

Freshly ground black pepper

2 tablespoons capers, drained and chopped

8 green olives, pitted and finely chopped

4 cornichons, finely chopped

Flaky salt to taste

FOR THE GREEN OIL (OPTIONAL)

Reserved leek tops, cleaned

½ cup olive oil

1. PREPARE THE LEEKS AND EGGS: Remove the tough outer layers of the leeks and cut off the root ends. Slice the leeks lengthwise and place them in a large basin of warm water, swishing them vigorously to dislodge any sand or dirt. Remove them to a bowl or plate.

2. Prepare an ice water bath. In a large saucepan of salted boiling water, briskly simmer the leeks for 8 to 10 minutes, until they are fork-tender. Transfer them to the ice water bath.

3. Lower the eggs into the same simmering water and cook for 11 minutes. Transfer them to the ice water bath along with the leeks.

4. MEANWHILE, MAKE THE VINAIGRETTE FOR THE EGGS: In a small bowl whisk together the mustard and vinegar until smooth. Slowly whisk in the olive oil to make a thick sauce. Season with kosher salt and pepper to taste. Set aside.

5. IF YOU'RE MAKING THE GREEN OIL: Blanch the leek tops for 90 seconds in boiling water, then shock them in ice water. Pat dry and transfer to a blender. Add the olive oil and blend until smooth. Strain the mixture through a fine-mesh sieve or cheesecloth (the latter will be a bit less messy). The green oil will keep in the refrigerator for about 2 weeks.

6. Blot the leeks dry and plate them. Peel the eggs and break them with the back of a fork into small pieces. Drizzle the egg pieces lightly with vinaigrette. Sprinkle the leeks with the dressed egg pieces, the capers, olives, and cornichons. Finish with a drizzle of the green oil (if using) and a sprinkle of flaky salt and pepper.

I love to keep the root ends of
leeks for display and drama.

GRILLED SARDINES

SERVES 4 • **PREP TIME:** 5 MINUTES • **COOK TIME:** 5 MINUTES

Fresh sardines are a fleeting treasure at markets in the United States in the spring and summer—if you spot some with bright eyes and shiny skin, do not hesitate to buy them. They need nothing more than good olive oil, salt, and herbs. Eat them immediately, while they're still crisp.

1 pound (450 g) fresh sardines (12 to 16 sardines), cleaned

Olive oil

Flaky salt

1 lemon

Handful of flat-leaf parsley, roughly chopped

1. Heat the grill until very hot.

2. Brush the sardines with oil, and season them with flaky salt. Grill 2 minutes per side, until the skin is crisp and the flesh easily pulls away from the bones. The fish are fragile and may start to break, and that's okay.

3. Transfer the sardines to a platter. Drizzle them with the juice of half of the lemon, scatter them with parsley, and sprinkle them with more flaky salt.

4. Slice the other half of the lemon into wedges and serve immediately with the sardines.

GREEN FRITTATA

SERVES 4 TO 6 • **PREP TIME:** 15 MINUTES • **COOK TIME:** 25 MINUTES

A good frittata is the perfect solution for using up all those herbs wilting in your refrigerator; I always seem to have a few sprigs of something left over from the week's cooking. Mixed with eggs and a generous handful of cheese, even the most tired-looking vegetables transform into a fluffy, golden dish that's equally good hot from the oven or at room temperature. Think of this recipe as a template: Any combination of greens and herbs will work wonderfully as long as you don't skimp on the dairy.

6 eggs (for a 10-inch skillet) or 8 eggs (for a 12-inch skillet)

¼ cup (60 ml) whole milk

2 garlic cloves, minced

Kosher salt

2 tablespoons olive oil

4 scallions, thinly sliced

A bunch of asparagus spears, cut into 1-inch pieces (about ½ cup / 70 g)

½ cup (70 g) frozen peas

1 cup (100 g) grated Parmesan, Gruyère, small-diced mozzarella, or crumbled feta

½ cup (20 g) finely chopped mixed herbs, such as tarragon leaves, chives, thyme leaves, and parsley

Freshly ground black pepper

1. Preheat the oven to 400°F.

2. In a large bowl, whisk together the eggs, milk, garlic, and 1 teaspoon salt until well combined.

3. In a 10- or 12-inch oven-safe skillet, heat the olive oil over medium heat. Add the scallions, asparagus, and a pinch of salt. Cook, stirring occasionally, until the asparagus is tender but still bright green, about 5 minutes. Add the peas and cook until they are warmed through, about 3 minutes. Spread the vegetables evenly across the bottom of the pan.

4. Pour the egg mixture into the pan and shake gently to distribute evenly. Scatter the cheese over the top and sprinkle with the mixed herbs. Transfer to the oven and bake until the frittata is just set but still slightly jiggly in the center, 15 to 20 minutes.

5. Let rest for 5 minutes—the residual heat will finish cooking the center. The frittata can be served hot, while still puffed up, or at room temperature. Finish with a few grindings of pepper and cut into wedges for serving.

TRADITIONAL FRENCH OMELETTE

SERVES 1 • **PREP TIME:** 5 MINUTES • **COOK TIME:** 5 MINUTES

Learning to make eggs is a lifelong gift to yourself, and others. Whenever I visit my family in France, I become the designated egg cook. It's a ritual I really enjoy—everyone shuffling into the kitchen in the morning, waiting for their turn. While they're mainly a breakfast item here, omelettes are a fine appetizer or lazy lunch in France. On a bed of greens, it's an elegant meal at your fingertips.

3 large eggs, at room temperature

¼ teaspoon kosher salt

2½ tablespoons unsalted butter

¼ cup (10 g) chopped fresh herbs, such as chives, parsley, or tarragon

1. In a medium bowl, whisk together the eggs and salt until thoroughly combined, with no streaks of egg white remaining.

2. Heat an 8-inch nonstick skillet over medium heat until hot. Add 2 tablespoons of the butter and swirl until the foaming subsides. Pour in the eggs—they should sizzle immediately on contact. Let them cook undisturbed until the bottom just sets, 20 to 30 seconds.

3. Reduce the heat to low. Using a heatproof spatula, constantly push the edges of the eggs toward the center, tilting the pan to let raw egg flow to the edges. You're looking for soft, creamy curds—think tiny pillows rather than scrambled eggs.

4. When the eggs are mostly set but still look a bit wet on top, 1 to 2 minutes, use a spatula to smooth them into an even layer. The edges should be set but the center should still have some movement.

5. Tilt the pan away from you at a 45-degree angle. Use your spatula to lift the edge closest to you and gently roll the omelette onto itself, creating a seam at the bottom. Spread the remaining ½ tablespoon of butter over the top. The omelette should be pale gold on the outside, with no browning, and creamy but fully set in the center.

6. Tilt the omelette onto a warm plate, seam side down. Shower with fresh herbs and serve immediately.

PIPÉRADE

SERVES 4 • **PREP TIME:** 15 MINUTES • **COOK TIME:** 45 MINUTES

I learned while writing this book that pipérade is a Basque dish of peppers and eggs. In my house, it was always shorthand for any vegetable or ratatouille leftovers revived with eggs cracked on top, a little bit like a shakshuka. The traditional version uses Espelette pepper, but regular red pepper flakes work too. Whatever you do, serve it with good bread for soaking up the jammy peppers and runny yolks.

3 yellow onions, sliced into half-moons

¼ cup (60 ml) olive oil, plus more for drizzling

6 mixed bell peppers (any color), cored, seeded and cut into 1-inch strips

1 teaspoon sugar

4 garlic cloves, sliced

4 thyme sprigs

4 ripe tomatoes, roughly chopped

1 teaspoon kosher salt

6 eggs

1 teaspoon salt

Freshly ground black pepper to taste

½ teaspoon Espelette pepper or other red pepper flakes

1 small bunch curly parsley, chopped

1. In a large skillet over medium-low heat, combine the onions with 2 tablespoons of the olive oil. Let them cook gently until slightly browned, stirring occasionally, about 8 minutes.

Add the peppers and sugar and cook them slowly, stirring often, until the onions and peppers are caramelized, about 15 minutes. Add the garlic, thyme sprigs, and tomatoes and cook until everything is soft and jammy, about 30 minutes. You can cover the pan to speed the cooking, but you want most of the juice from the tomatoes to evaporate. Remove the thyme sprigs.

2. Make six wells in the mixture and crack an egg into each. Reduce heat to low and cover the pan and cook until the whites are fully set but the yolks are still runny, about 3 minutes.

3. Finish with a drizzle of oil, the salt, black pepper, and Espelette pepper. Garnish with the parsley and serve.

> **NOTE:** *Any leftover vegetables work here— just get them hot and jammy before adding the eggs.*

MOM'S QUICHE

SERVES 4 TO 6 • **PREP TIME:** 10 MINUTES (WITH PREMADE PASTRY CRUST)
COOK TIME: 35 MINUTES

In France, quiche isn't breakfast food—it's what we make when we need to warm up the house at lunchtime. This version is my favorite, with salty lardons melted into a silky custard and plenty of Gruyère forming a golden crust on top, though it's also perfect for transforming leftover vegetables into lunch. Just don't skimp on the dairy—it's what makes the quiche light and puffy.

1 store-bought pastry crust or 1 Pâte Brisée (page 14)

7 ounces (200 g) lardons or thick-cut ham

6 large eggs

½ cup (120 ml) heavy cream

¼ teaspoon freshly ground black pepper

Pinch of freshly grated nutmeg (optional)

1 cup (115 g) grated Gruyère

1. Preheat the oven to 400°F.

2. Line an 11-inch quiche dish or pie plate with the pastry.

3. In a medium skillet over medium heat, cook the lardons, stirring occasionally, until they just start to brown and render their fat, about 5 minutes.

4. In a large bowl, whisk together the eggs, cream, pepper, and nutmeg (if using). Stir in ⅓ cup of the Gruyère and the warm lardons. Pour the egg mixture into the pastry shell and sprinkle the remaining ⅔ cup cheese over the top.

5. Bake until the quiche is puffed and golden brown, about 35 minutes. Let rest for a few minutes, then cut into wedges. For an accompaniment, serve with Green Salad with Mustard Vinaigrette (page 75).

SALADS

Wherever I am, no place takes me home
like the farmers' market.

In France we just call it the market.

"ALL THE GREEN THINGS" SHAVED SALAD

SERVES 4 TO 6 • **PREP TIME:** 20 MINUTES

This is the salad I make when summer hits and cooking feels impossible. The recipe features sharp vegetables made soft through careful slicing, and a dressing of good olive oil and fresh lemon juice. Be careful and use a mandoline or a very sharp knife.

1 lemon

6 baby artichokes

2 fennel bulbs (a handful of fronds reserved, optional)

4 celery stalks (a handful of leaves reserved, optional)

⅓ cup (80 ml) olive oil

Flaky salt

1 bunch flat-leaf parsley, roughly chopped

2 ounces (57 g) aged Parmesan, shaved or grated

2 tablespoons capers, drained and smashed

Optional garnishes: pink peppercorns, toasted pine nuts, reserved fennel fronds and celery leaves, and/or edible flowers, if available

1. Zest the lemon and set aside the zest. Fill a large bowl with the cold water and add the juice from half of the lemon.

2. Strip the outer leaves from the artichokes until you reach the pale, tender ones. Cut off the top third of the artichokes and slice them paper-thin on the mandoline lengthwise (from top to bottom), then immediately drop them into the lemon water. This will keep them from turning brown before you use them.

3. Using the mandoline, shave the fennel and celery very thinly.

4. Drain the artichokes and pat dry. Dry the bowl well and combine the juice from the remaining lemon half, the zest, oil, and a generous pinch of flaky salt. Add the shaved artichokes, fennel, celery, and parsley and toss gently to coat.

5. Arrange the vegetables on a platter. Top with the Parmesan, smashed capers, and a scattering of any of the garnishes (if using).

DON'T BE SCARED OF ARTICHOKES

Artichokes are just flowers with an attitude; they have thorns and make you work for their hearts. But once you learn the few simple moves to dismantle them, many bright spring salads, crispy fried leaves, and tender hearts await on the other side of these few basic knife skills. If you're lucky enough to find the tiny purple artichokes of the Riviera, you can shave them raw into salads—they're tender enough to eat whole, no dismantling required.

1. Pull off the tough outer leaves at the base. They'll snap off easily—if they don't, they're too tough to eat.

2. Cut off the top third of the artichoke, where the leaves come to a point.

3. Using kitchen scissors, snip the thorny tips off the remaining outer leaves.

4. Trim the stem, leaving about 2 inches. Use a vegetable peeler to remove the tough outer layer—the inside is tender and edible.

5. Cut the artichoke in half lengthwise.

6. Remove the fuzzy choke in the center using a small spoon, scraping it out completely.

7. Rub the cut surfaces with lemon to prevent browning, or drop the artichoke halves into lemony water if not cooking immediately.

WAX BEAN AND HARICOT VERT SALAD WITH FETA DRESSING

SERVES 4 TO 6 • **PREP TIME:** 15 MINUTES • **COOK TIME:** 5 MINUTES

Yellow beans are a staple of the Riviera, piled high at every market stand all summer long—and they're deeply nostalgic for me now that I'm far from home. This feta dressing is a family shortcut I've carried with me, simple enough that it hardly counts as a recipe. The salty cheese mellowed with lemon works its way into so many of my meals: tossed with any vegetable that needs brightening, spread thickly on bread, or spooned over grilled fish on lazy evenings.

FOR THE BEANS

¾ pound (340 g) wax beans

¾ pound (340 g) haricots verts

Large handful of basil leaves

Flaky salt

FOR THE FETA DRESSING

1 tablespoon finely minced shallot

2 garlic cloves, minced

Zest and juice of 1 lemon, plus more as needed, or 2 to 3 tablespoons cured lemon juice (see page 10)

Kosher salt

7 ounces (200 g) feta

¼ cup (60 ml) olive oil, plus more as needed

Freshly ground black pepper

1. PREPARE THE BEANS: Snap off the stem end of each bean and pull off any strings that come with it. Some people trim both ends, but I find the tender tip can stay. If any beans are particularly long, cut them in half on a diagonal—this creates a more elegant shape than straight across.

2. In a large bowl, prepare an ice water bath. Steam the beans for 2 to 3 minutes, until tender, crisp, and brightly colored. Remove the beans with a slotted spoon and transfer them to the ice water bath to stop the cooking and preserve their color.

3. PREPARE THE DRESSING: In a separate large bowl, combine the shallot, garlic, lemon zest and juice, and a pinch of salt. Let sit for 5 minutes to soften the shallot's bite. Crumble in the feta, add the olive oil, and stir until creamy. The dressing should be loose enough to coat a spoon—add more oil if needed. Taste for salt and acid and adjust as desired.

4. Add the cooled beans to the bowl with the feta dressing and toss gently to coat. Tear in the basil leaves, taste for salt, and finish with another drizzle of oil.

DAURADES AU VIN BLANC
● Pour 4 personnes : 2 daurades de 800 g environ, 2 verres de vin blanc, thym, laurier, fenouil, 4 tomates, 40 g de beurre, sel, poivre.
Pelez les daurades. Placez-les dans un plat à gratin beurré, avec les oignons coupés en rondelles. Disposez les tomates en petit morceaux avec le vin blanc, caramelisées. Mettez les daurades. Arrosez avec le vin blanc. Salez, poivrez. Faites cuire à four moyen pendant 30 minutes.

THON À LA PROVEN...

Faites cuire le tho...
sur table, avec du beur...
bien hachées ; saupou...
et faites lui prend...

RECETTES

Ne mettez jamais les moules dans l'eau, car elles rejettent la leur pour absorber de l'eau douce et perdent leur saveur ; ne faites jamais trop cuire les moules.

MOULES MARINIÈRES. — Mettez vos moules dans une casserole sur le feu vif avec le feu vif avec un demi-verre de vin blanc par litre de moules, échalotes, persil haché, poivre, thym, laurier. Couvrir et laisser prendre ébullition 4 à 5 minutes. Retirer les moules en enlevant une coquille, faire réduire la cuisson et le jus de citron. Verser devant être onctueuse, la répandra en...

MOULES POULETTE. — Même préparation que la moule marinière, mais la sauce devant être onctueuse, la faire cuire préparant un léger roux blanc avec un peu de fécule, beurre et fus de moules. Mouiller ce roux avec les moules, laisser cuire la sauce dix minutes environ, puis lier avec un peu de farine par litre de moules. Mouiller d'un bon morceau de beurre frais, vinaigre ou citron si l'on veut, quelques cuillerées de crème double. Cette sauce étant pochée, la verser sur les moules ou 3 jaunes d'œufs, un bon morceau de beurre au moment de servir et saupoudrer le tout d'un peu de persil haché.

MOULES GRILLÉES. — Disposer les moules sur le gril et faire cuire. Servir très chaudes avec du beurre frais.

SALADE DE MOULES ET MOULES MAYONNAISE. — Faites ouvrir à sec dans une casserole bien couverte à feu vif. Sortir les moules de la coquille et mettre en salade avec moutarde, hachis d'ail et de persil ; ou servir avec une mayonnaise.

MOULES SAUTÉES AU BEURRE. — Faire ouvrir les coquilles et faites sauter les moules au beurre avec hachis d'échalotes et mettre en coquille. Couper en tranches de belles tomates. Faire fondre à la poêle un morceau de beurre, y mettre les moules et les couvrir de tranches de tomates. Mettre un couvercle et faire cuire à feu doux.

MOULES ROCHELAISE. — Faire ouvrir les moules. Las sortir de leur coquille. Les hacher avec un peu de persil et un peu en gros morceaux de beurre, à feu très vif. Sortir les moules, enlevez une coquille. Préparer une béchamelle assez épaisse, fromage de gruyère râpé et un jaune d'œuf battu et ensuite dans la chapelure. Faire cuire et le servir.

CROQUETTES DE MOULES. — Faire ouvrir les moules. Les sortir de leur coquille. Arrosez d'un petit verre de cognac et flambez. Mouiller ensuite dans la casserole un verre d'eau ou le bouillon des champignons de Paris qui auront fait blanchir à part, et un peu d'eau des moules ce qui suffira pour mettre la casserole doux en refroidir complètement. Former des croquettes, les rouler dans la farine, puis dans l'œuf battu et ensuite dans la chapelure. Faire frire à l'huile, laisser égoutter sur un linge et dresser sur un plat. Servir à part, faire revenir au beurre.

MOULES À LA FRANÇAISE. — Après avoir fait ouvrir les moules. Des qu'elles sont ouvertes, les enlever un bon morceau de beurre, un oignon et de persil hachés et laissez-les mijoter quelques minutes. D'autre part, faire revenir au beurre un bouquet garni, quelques échalotes émincées finement ; laisser revenir ce hachis dans une petite casserole, mouiller de la moitié de la cuisson ; mélanger ensuite avec les moules, y ajouter d'un jaune d'œuf. Servir garni, un bouquet garni, quelques échalotes émincées finement ; laisser...

MOUCLADE. — Faire blondir du beurre 50 grammes d'oignons hachés. Ajouter ce qu'il soit bien mordoré de beurre. Mouiller d'un quart... Former et bien mélange et faire prendre en tournant. Mouiller doucement avec de la crème poivrer, sortir dans un plat creux, saupoudrer le riz si le riz est son, disposer sur...

RIZOTTO AUX MOULES (proportions pour 5 personnes) : Faire blondir du beurre 50 grammes d'oignons hachés. Ajouter ce qu'il soit bien mordoré sur le feu dix minutes ; ajouter le riz et bien le rouler dans ce beurre. Après dix minutes, préparez le riz si le riz est son, disposer sur...

GREEN SALAD WITH MUSTARD VINAIGRETTE

SERVES 4 TO 6 • **PREP TIME:** 15 MINUTES

Every meal in my house begins this way—a pile of just-dressed greens in a big bowl, each leaf glossy with tangy vinaigrette. There are some key rules: Wet lettuce makes for a sad dressing, so make sure your lettuce is bone-dry before dressing it; and every leaf needs a light but even coat of vinaigrette. (the cookbook author Patricia Wells instructs us to toss a salad thirty-three times for best coverage). Take your time with the dressing and add more lettuce little by little—I'm a lazy cook who likes to save on washing: I make my dressing at the bottom of the salad bowl and add the salad on top. I miss the mâche from home, but any tender market greens will shine here. Be sure to let the shallots mellow in the vinegar first.

1 tablespoon red wine vinegar

½ shallot, finely minced

Pinch of kosher salt

Freshly ground black pepper

1 teaspoon Dijon mustard

¼ cup (60 ml) your best olive oil

8 cups (225 g) salad greens (mâche, butter lettuce, or young market greens), washed and very dry

Freshly ground black pepper

Flaky salt

1. Combine the vinegar, shallot, kosher salt and pepper in a serving bowl. Let rest for 10 minutes—this takes the bite out of the shallots. Whisk in the mustard, then slowly stream in the oil, whisking until emulsified.

2. Pile the greens on top of the dressing. Using your clean hands or salad servers, gently lift and turn the leaves until each one is lightly coated. Taste and add flaky salt and pepper as needed—you want every bite to be a little salty. Serve immediately.

SALADE NIÇOISE, MY WAY

SERVES 4 • **PREP TIME:** 10 MINUTES • **COOK TIME:** 25 MINUTES

This salad strays far from Nice's original—no lettuce, yes potatoes—but it's the kind of thing you can throw together from a well-stocked pantry and whatever's left from the market. The key is getting each element just right: potatoes still warm when they hit the olive oil, eggs with properly jammy centers, really good-quality tuna in oil. Purists prefer to use only lemon and oil to season this salad, but if I have leftover pesto on hand or a vinegar I really love, I never mind using a splash of those either.

1 garlic clove, halved

1 pint cherry tomatoes, halved lengthwise

Kosher salt

¾ pound (340 g) small waxy potatoes

½ pound (225 g) haricots verts, trimmed

2 eggs

⅓ cup (80 ml) your best olive oil, plus more for drizzling

Two 5-ounce cans best-quality tuna in olive oil, drained

½ red onion, very thinly sliced (if pickled, even better)

¼ cup (35 g) caper berries

⅓ cup (45 g) pitted or unpitted Niçoise olives

1 lemon, halved

Freshly ground black pepper to taste

1. Rub the inside of a wide serving bowl thoroughly with the garlic halves. Place the tomatoes in a medium bowl and lightly sprinkle them with salt. Set aside.

2. Fill a medium pot with salted water and bring it to a boil over medium-high heat—we'll use this for all the cooking. First, add the potatoes and cook until a knife slides in easily,

12 to 15 minutes. Remove them with a slotted spoon and set aside.

3. Next, cook the beans for 3 minutes, until tender but still with a snap. While the beans are cooking, in a large bowl prepare an ice water bath. Using a slotted spoon, transfer the cooked beans to the ice water bath to stop the cooking. Once cool, scoop them out and set them aside (keep the bowl of ice water).

4. Finally, cook the eggs—I like them jammy, so I set a timer for 7 minutes from the second they get into the boiling water. Transfer them to the ice water bath until cool, then peel and halve the eggs.

5. Layer the warm potatoes in the garlic-rubbed serving bowl, drizzling with the olive oil and lightly sprinkling with salt as you go. Arrange the tomatoes, beans, eggs, tuna, red onion, caper berries, and olives in sections.

6. Grill the lemon halves cut side down until charred, about 2 minutes. Squeeze lemon juice over the salad, drizzle generously with olive oil, and season with pepper.

MOZZARELLA, PEAS, AND GREENS SOTT'OLIO

SERVES 4 TO 6 • **PREP TIME:** 15 MINUTES (AN EXTRA 20 TO 60 MINUTES FOR MARINATING IS GREAT BUT NOT NECESSARY) • **COOK TIME:** 3 MINUTES

This is barely a recipe—just good mozzarella bathed in olive oil with tender greens and peas—yet it shows up on my table over and over again. Fresh peas are a spring treasure, but I use frozen ones the rest of the year. Either way, you want plenty of oil for the cheese to swim in—you'll end up chasing it around the plate when the mozzarella is long gone.

Kosher salt

2 cups (300 g) fresh peas, or 1 cup (150 g) frozen

2 bunches Swiss chard or other tender greens

Two 4-ounce balls fresh mozzarella or burrata

⅓ cup olives, pitted or unpitted

½ cup (120 ml) your best olive oil, plus more for serving

Flaky salt and freshly ground black pepper to taste

1. Bring a large pot of water seasoned with kosher salt to a boil. Cook the peas until tender, about 4 minutes for fresh and 2 minutes for frozen, remove with a slotted spoon, and set aside. Keep the water boiling.

2. Strip the chard leaves from their stems and tear them into large pieces. In the same water, blanch the chard leaves until just wilted, about 1 minute. Drain and gently squeeze dry.

3. Tear the mozzarella into large chunks.

4. Arrange the chard, peas, mozzarella, and olives on a platter with a slight lip. Pour the oil on top. I like to let this dish sit for at least 20 minutes for the greens and cheese to soak up the oil—a nice step if you have the time.

5. Season with some flaky salt and pepper, finish with more oil, and serve.

The stunning Hôtel du Couvent in Nice.

MELON SALAD WITH MINT AND PECORINO

SERVES 4 TO 6 • **PREP TIME:** 15 MINUTES

Sweet, fragrant melon is traditionally wrapped in prosciutto for every lunch of the summer in Provence. But something magical happens when peak-ripe melon meets olive oil and salt. It's a dance of contrasts: cold, crisp melon against shards of aged cheese, sweet and salty bites that come together in minutes in a dish that is refreshing but substantial.

1 ripe cantaloupe (a honeydew melon works well here too)

2 ounces (60 g) aged pecorino or any cheese firm enough not to crumble when shaved into curls

2 small Persian cucumbers

⅓ cup lightly packed mint leaves

3 tablespoons your best olive oil

1 lime (optional)

Flaky salt and freshly ground black pepper

1. Cut the melon in half lengthwise and remove the seeds. Cut the flesh into slices—I prefer these to cubes, as they are more elegant and catch more of the dressing.

2. Using a vegetable peeler, shave the cheese into delicate curls. Slice the cucumbers into ¼-inch-thick slices. Tear the mint leaves, reserving a few whole ones for garnish.

3. Arrange the melon and cucumbers on a large platter. Scatter with cheese shavings and torn mint. Just before serving, drizzle generously with olive oil and squeeze the lime (if using) on top. Finish with some flaky salt and black pepper.

> **NOTE:** *The key here is using a perfectly ripe melon. If your melon isn't quite at its peak, let it ripen at room temperature for a day or two, or mix a couple drops of honey with the olive oil. A ripe melon should feel heavy for its size and smell sweetly fragrant, almost musky at the stem end.*

CARROT SALAD WITH MINT AND CRUSHED ALMONDS

SERVES 4 TO 6 • **PREP TIME:** 15 MINUTES

A box grater makes quick work of carrots, but I prefer to take my time with a sharp knife here, cutting them into thin matchsticks that catch the dressing in their corners. Like many dishes from the Riviera, this salad nods to North African flavors—the orange and coriander in the dressing and a drizzle of harissa or spicy oil if you're feeling bold. The mint and almonds make this dish feel delicate yet hearty.

⅓ cup (30 g) sliced almonds

6 large carrots

Juice of ½ orange

2 tablespoons white wine vinegar

Flaky salt

3 tablespoons your best olive oil

1 teaspoon harissa or chili oil

1 teaspoon crushed coriander seeds (optional)

⅓ cup mint leaves, roughly torn

Freshly ground black pepper to taste

Zest of ½ orange

1. Toast the almonds in a dry pan over medium heat until golden, taking care not to burn them. Set aside to cool.

2. Cut the carrots into fine matchsticks or use a peeler to make long ribbons.

3. In a large bowl, combine the orange juice, vinegar, and a pinch of salt. Whisk in the harissa oil and the coriander (if using). Add the carrots, mint, and most of the almonds. Toss gently until everything is glossy with dressing. Season with salt and pepper.

4. Arrange on a platter and scatter the remaining almonds and the orange zest.

ARTICHOKE AND BEAN SALAD

SERVES 4 TO 6 • **PREP TIME:** 10 MINUTES

A can of beans, some jarred artichokes, good olive oil—this is assembly rather than cooking, but it transports me straight to long summer lunches in Europe, even if all the ingredients came from my pantry. Make it your own with whatever treasures you have on hand: Garlic Confit (page 2), chopped Cured Lemons (page 10), some pickles. It's perfect as a side dish but substantial and nutritious enough for a solo dinner eaten straight from the bowl.

Juice of 1 lemon, plus more if needed

2 teaspoons Dijon mustard

Flaky salt

⅓ cup (80 ml) your best olive oil, plus more if needed

Two 14-ounce cans (680 g) white (cannellini) beans, drained

Two 10-ounce jars (450 g) marinated artichoke hearts, drained

One 10-ounce jar (225 g) roasted red peppers, drained and torn into small strips

Handful of parsley, savory, or dill

Freshly ground black pepper

1. In a large bowl, whisk together the lemon juice, mustard, and a pinch of salt. Slowly stream in the oil. Add the beans, artichokes, and peppers and toss gently. Let sit 10 minutes for the flavors to meld.

2. Tear the herbs and add to the bowl. Taste and add more salt and/or lemon juice if desired. Finish with pepper and more oil as needed.

SOUPS

My grandmother Mymo, great-grandmother Nenette,
and me in front of the beach we used to go to every
single morning, though not always in matching
shoes. When people ask me about my dream for Ghia,
I always say: for Ghia to be everywhere, even the
kiosk in front of Bijou Plage.

GAZPACHO

SERVES 4 • **PREP TIME:** 5 MINUTES PLUS CHILLING • **COOK TIME:** 10 MINUTES

The beauty of gazpacho lies in its simplicity—everything goes into the blender, no cooking required. While it's perfectly lovely on its own, I can never resist topping with garlicky croutons, a shower of diced cucumber, and fluffy egg mimosa (see page 54). On the hottest summer days, there's nothing more refreshing. The main ingredient here is tomatoes, so use the most flavorful ones you can find (it's okay if they're a little soft).

FOR THE SOUP

2 pounds (1 kg) ripe tomatoes, cored and cut into large chunks

1 red bell pepper, cored, seeded, and roughly chopped

1 garlic clove

¼ cup (60 ml) olive oil, plus more for serving

2 tablespoons sherry vinegar

Kosher salt

Freshly ground black pepper

TOPPINGS

2 eggs

2 tablespoons olive oil

2 thick slices country bread

1 garlic clove, smashed

1 small cucumber, finely diced

Your best olive oil

Fresh herbs, such as basil or parsley (optional)

1. PREPARE THE SOUP: In a blender, combine the tomatoes, bell pepper, garlic, oil, and vinegar and blend on high speed until very smooth. Season generously with salt and pepper, pour into a serving pitcher, and place in the refrigerator to chill until it's time to eat.

2. PREPARE THE TOPPINGS: In a large bowl, prepare an ice water bath. Bring a small saucepan of water to a boil. Carefully lower the eggs into the boiling water and cook for 9 minutes. Remove the eggs with a slotted spoon and transfer to the ice water bath to stop the cooking.

3. While the eggs are cooling, make the croutons. In a medium sauté pan, heat the olive oil over medium heat. Add the bread and toast on both sides until golden and crisp, 2 to 3 minutes per side. Remove from the heat, then rub the toasts with the garlic clove while still hot. Cut the toasts into croutons.

4. Peel the eggs and, with the back of a fork, break the eggs into small pieces (this is your egg mimosa, as seen on page 55).

5. Serve the gazpacho cold, topped with cucumber, croutons, and egg mimosa. Finish with a drizzle of your best olive oil and a sprinkling of herbs of your choice (if using).

COLD PEA AND MINT SOUP

SERVES 4 TO 6 • **PREP TIME:** 10 MINUTES • **COOK TIME:** 20 MINUTES PLUS 2 HOURS CHILLING

Fresh peas are one of spring's sweetest gifts, though since they have such a short season I often rely on frozen. Either way, they become velvety and sweet here, brightened with herbs and good olive oil. Serving them alongside feta-topped toast creates something magical. The contrast of temperature and texture—cold, silky soup, warm bread, salty cheese—makes this dish feel far more sophisticated than its humble ingredients suggest.

FOR THE SOUP

1 shallot, finely chopped

2 tablespoons butter

2 garlic cloves, minced

2 pounds (900 g) fresh or frozen peas

Handful of mint leaves, plus more for garnish

8 basil leaves

4 cups (1 L) vegetable broth, homemade (see page 6) or store-bought

¼ cup (60 ml) olive oil

Kosher salt to taste

Freshly ground white pepper, to taste (optional)

FETA TOASTS

4 thick slices country bread

Your best olive oil, for drizzling

7 ounces (200 g) Greek feta

Handful of pistachios, for garnish

1. PREPARE THE SOUP: In a medium stockpot, melt the butter over medium heat. Add the shallot and sauté until soft and translucent, about 5 minutes. Add the garlic and sauté until fragrant, 1 to 2 minutes. Add the peas (if using fresh) and all the broth. Simmer for 10 minutes, until tender. (If using frozen peas, simmer for 2 minutes.) Remove from the heat and stir in half the mint and basil leaves.

2. Transfer the soup to a blender or food processor and blend until very smooth and creamy, streaming in the olive oil as you blend. Take care, as the soup will be hot. It might take a few minutes of blending to achieve a truly silky texture. Season well with salt and white pepper (if using). Chill thoroughly in the refrigerator for at least 2 hours before serving.

3. PREPARE THE FETA TOASTS: Toast the bread, then drizzle it with some of your best olive oil. Crumble the feta on top.

4. When the soup has chilled, garnish with the pistachios, some mint leaves, and a drizzle of your best olive oil. Serve with the feta toast alongside. The soup will keep for 2 days in the refrigerator. Cover with plastic wrap pressed directly onto the surface to maintain its bright color.

SOUPE AU PISTOU

FRENCH MINESTRONE

SERVES 6 • **PREP TIME:** 15 MINUTES • **COOK TIME:** 45 MINUTES

This is the Riviera's version of a minestrone—a celebration of summer vegetables and herbs that somehow manages to be both light and satisfying. While some versions start with dried beans that need overnight soaking, I prefer small red beans and white coco beans, which cook right alongside the vegetables. The real magic happens when you swirl in the pistou at the end—watch it create bright green rivulets through the golden broth.

3 tablespoons olive oil

2 garlic cloves

2 yellow onions, cut into small dice

2 carrots, cut into small dice

2 zucchini, cut into small dice

½ pound (225 g) haricots verts, trimmed

½ cup (100 g) dried small red beans

½ cup (100 g) dried white coco beans

2 teaspoons kosher salt

Freshly ground black pepper

2 small potatoes, cut into ½-inch dice

1 cup (100 g) elbow pasta

Freshly grated Parmesan, for serving

Pistou (recipe follows), for serving

1. In a large Dutch oven or other heavy pot, heat the olive oil over medium heat. Add the garlic, onions, carrots, zucchini, and haricots verts and let the vegetables get acquainted—cook until they start to soften and become fragrant, about 8 minutes. Add both types of dried beans, season with the salt and a generous amount of pepper, and add water to cover. Bring to a gentle simmer and cook for 20 minutes, until the beans are just tender.

2. Add the diced potatoes and cook for 15 minutes, until they pierce easily with a fork, then add the pasta and cook until it is al dente, about 10 minutes.

3. Serve hot, with freshly grated Parmesan and generous spoonful of pistou swirled into each bowl—and extra for passing at the table, because someone always wants more.

PISTOU

FRENCH PESTO

MAKES ABOUT 1 CUP • **PREP TIME:** 10 MINUTES • **COOK TIME:** 10 MINUTES

Pistou is the French version of Italian pesto. Both start with crushed basil and garlic, but pistou traditionally skips the pine nuts, letting the basil shine more brightly. Every summer of my childhood, I'd watch my grandmother make it, sitting in her garden with a mortar and pestle, crushing basil leaves into a fragrant paste. While a food processor makes quick work of it, doing it by hand lets the basil release its oils more slowly, creating deeper, more complex flavors. But honestly, even blended pistou is leagues better than no pistou at all.

1 large garlic clove

¼ cup pine nuts

Pinch of kosher salt

2 cups (40 g) fresh basil leaves

¼ cup (60 ml) your best olive oil, plus more as needed for storage

1½ ounce (45 g) Parmesan

1. If using a mortar and pestle, pound the garlic, pine nuts, and salt into a smooth paste. Roughly chop the basil leaves and pound them into the garlic paste until dark green and smooth. Slowly drizzle in the olive oil while pounding. Grate the Parmesan and incorporate to finish.

2. If using a food processor, pulse the garlic, salt, and basil until finely chopped. With the motor running, drizzle in the oil. Add the Parmesan and pulse to combine. Fresh pistou will keep for several days in an airtight container in the refrigerator if fully submerged in olive oil.

AIGO BOULIDO

PROVENÇAL GARLIC SOUP

SERVES 4 • **PREP TIME:** 15 MINUTES • **COOK TIME:** 20 MINUTES

Boulido means "boiled water" in Provençal, but don't let that fool you—this is a deeply aromatic broth of garlic and herbs, enriched with egg and served over crusty bread. It's what we make when one is sick: infused garlic and herb broth with a crispy toast, accompanied by a warm blanket and a little nap. Simple as this soup is, there's something incredibly restorative about it.

1 garlic head

1 thyme sprig

1 bay leaf

2 teaspoons kosher salt

1 small bunch sage

4 slices country bread

4 eggs

Your best olive oil, for drizzling

Freshly ground black pepper

1. Separate the garlic cloves and peel them, without removing the germ if there is one.

2. In a large saucepan, combine the garlic, thyme, bay leaf, salt, and 4 cups (1 L) water. Bring to a simmer over medium heat and cook gently for 10 minutes. Remove the garlic with a slotted spoon, add the sage (reserving a few leaves for serving), cover, and turn off the heat. Let infuse for 10 minutes. Mash the cooked garlic with a fork on a cutting board.

3. Toast the bread and place it in serving bowls. Separate the egg yolks from the whites—no need for a perfect split. Drizzle an egg yolk over each piece of toast (or serve it whole, as in the photo, if you feel adventurous) and top with a generous drizzle of olive oil.

4. Remove the herbs from the broth, stir in the mashed garlic, and bring the soup back to a gentle simmer. Turn off the heat. Whisk the egg whites, then slowly stir them in to create delicate ribbons.

5. Ladle the hot soup over the bread and yolks. Finish with the reserved sage leaves, some pepper, and another drizzle of oil.

> **NOTE:** *This traditional version calls for raw egg yolks, so use the freshest eggs possible. For an easy adaptation, you can drop whisked eggs into the simmering broth instead, creating a heartier soup with fully cooked eggs.*

SOUPE DE POISSON

SERVES 6 • **PREP TIME:** 30 MINUTES • **COOK TIME:** 1 HOUR

Of all the dishes from the French Riviera, this rich fish soup might be my favorite—and it's one that, mysteriously, hasn't found fame beyond our shores. The rust-colored broth, thick enough to coat a spoon, is served with golden croutons slathered in garlicky rouille and a generous sprinkling of Gruyère. It's a humble dish at heart, made from fish heads and bones that transform into an extraordinary sea-kissed broth.

2 pounds (900 g) mixed whitefish scraps, bones, and heads, such as from monkfish, snapper, sea bass, halibut (see Note, page 100)

2 yellow onions

2 leeks, white parts only, cleaned

2 carrots

2 celery stalks

4 garlic cloves

2 tomatoes, cored

¼ cup (60 ml) olive oil

1 tablespoon tomato paste

½ pound (225 g) shrimp shells and heads (from your fishmonger)

2 strips orange peel

Pinch of saffron threads

1 bay leaf

2 thyme sprigs

1 cup (240 ml) dry white wine

2 teaspoons kosher salt

Freshly ground black pepper

FOR SERVING

12 baguette slices

Rouille Provençale (recipe follows)

1 cup (100 g) grated Gruyère

1. Remove any gills from the fish heads—they can make the broth bitter. Roughly chop the onions, leeks, carrots, celery, garlic, and tomatoes (no need to be too precise; they will all be blended).

2. In a large Dutch oven or other heavy pot, heat the olive oil over medium heat. Add the onions, leeks, carrots, and celery and cook until they soften and become fragrant, stirring often, about 8 minutes. Add the garlic, tomatoes, and tomato paste and cook, stirring, until the tomato paste darkens slightly, about 2 minutes.

3. Add the fish pieces, shrimp shells and heads, orange peel, saffron, herbs, and wine. Bring to a simmer for about a minute, then add

Continues

6 cups (1.5 L) water. Bring to a gentle simmer and cook, partially covered, for 45 minutes. The broth will turn a deep golden orange.

4. Working in batches, blend the soup in a high-powered blender until very smooth— be careful, it's hot. Pass the soup through a fine-mesh sieve, pressing firmly to extract all the flavor. Return the soup to the pot and simmer until it is thick enough to coat the back of a spoon. Add the salt and season with pepper.

5. Meanwhile, slice and toast the baguette until golden. Serve the soup piping hot with rouille-slathered croutons floating on top and plenty of Gruyère to sprinkle.

> **NOTE:** *Ask your fishmonger for fish heads and bones—they'll give your soup its deepest flavor. Everything gets strained out, so you're not eating them directly, just extracting their essence for the broth. The broth can be made a day ahead and reheated gently.*

ROUILLE PROVENÇALE

SAFFRON AIOLI

Traditional rouille sometimes includes fish liver and is more of a rustic paste, but this golden, saffron-scented version is what most of us make today—and the version you'll want to slather generously on the croutons floating in your Soupe de Poisson (page 98). It's essentially a flavored aioli, with a little more heat, body, and complexity; the saffron gives it that beautiful sunset color and makes it feel special and distinctly Provençal.

Pinch of saffron threads

2 tablespoons warm water

2 garlic cloves

½ teaspoon flaky salt, plus more as needed

2 tablespoons fine bread crumbs

1 teaspoon Dijon mustard

2 egg yolks

1 tablespoon fresh lemon juice, plus more as needed

¾ cup (180 ml) your best olive oil

Pinch of cayenne pepper, plus more as needed

1. In a small bowl, steep the saffron in the warm water for 10 minutes to release its color and flavor.

2. Using a mortar and pestle, crush the garlic with the flaky salt into a smooth paste. Add the bread crumbs and continue grinding until you have a thick paste. If you don't have a mortar and pestle, you can use a food processor: Pulse the garlic, salt, and bread crumbs until you have a fine paste. Or you can mash everything together with the back of a fork in a medium bowl until well combined.

3. Add the mustard, egg yolks, lemon juice, and saffron with its soaking liquid and mix until well combined. If using a mortar, continue grinding; if using a bowl, whisk vigorously.

4. Begin adding the olive oil drop by drop, mixing constantly. When the mixture starts to thicken (after a few tablespoons of the oil), you can add the remaining oil in a thin, steady stream while continuing to mix vigorously.

5. When all the oil is incorporated, mix in the cayenne. You will have a thick, golden-orange sauce with a slightly rustic texture. Taste and adjust seasoning with more salt, lemon juice, or cayenne as needed.

6. Serve immediately with Soupe de Poisson or store the rouille in an airtight container in the refrigerator for up to 3 days.

PASTINA

SERVES 4 • **PREP TIME:** 10 MINUTES • **COOK TIME:** 35 MINUTES

While Italian grandmothers might have debated the perfect pastina shape (tiny stars! alphabets! little balls!), they all agreed that this soup has healing powers. The trick here is pureeing the vegetables right into the broth—they disappear completely and add velvety richness and nutrition. It's what I make when someone needs taking care of.

1 yellow onion, cut into chunks

2 carrots, scrubbed and cut into chunks

2 celery stalks, cut into chunks

6 cups chicken broth, homemade (see page 6) or store-bought

Parmesan rind (optional)

1½ cups tiny pasta, such as pastina, alphabet, or stelline

¼ cup parsley leaves

Freshly grated Parmesan

Kosher salt and freshly ground black pepper to taste

1. Cut the vegetables into chunks—they'll be pureed later, so no need to be too precise. Add them to a large pot with the broth and Parmesan rind (if using; if your broth is homemade, perhaps the flavor is already infused in). Bring the mixture to a boil over medium-high heat, then lower the heat to a simmer and cover. Cook gently until the vegetables are very tender, about 25 minutes.

2. Remove the Parmesan rind (if used). Using a slotted spoon, scoop the vegetables into a blender and add a couple ladles of broth. Blend until smooth—be careful, it's hot—then stir the puree back into the pot. Bring the mixture to a boil and add the pasta. Cook until the pasta is tender, about 3 minutes.

3. Taste the broth and season with salt and pepper. Serve the soup hot in bowls, topped with the parsley and plenty of grated Parmesan.

> **NOTE:** *The soup will thicken as it sits because the pasta continues to drink up the broth. Add a splash of hot water when reheating leftovers.*

MAKE IT YOUR OWN

For a grown-up summer version, add a pinch of saffron to the broth and stir in halved Sungold yellow cherry tomatoes just before serving. They burst into the broth, creating little pockets of sweet-tart brightness.

PASTA

Mymo and me. I only ever knew my grandmother to have jet-black hair.

My grandmother, my sister Manon, and me, eating again!

MAKING FRESH PASTA

I, too, used to be convinced that making fresh pasta required some kind of special skill I didn't possess. Yet it's flour, eggs, and maybe twenty minutes of your time that becomes one of the most forgiving, affordable, and generous meals you can make.

You really can't mess it up—add a little more flour if the dough is sticky, a splash of water if it's dry. It's hard to overknead and hard to overcook. Even the most uneven, wonky shapes taste infinitely better than anything from a box, and I've come to love the way kneading the dough seems to knead away whatever stress I brought with me into the kitchen. I love how it helps me slow down.

Now, when I'm having people over, I'll make the dough the night before, let it sleep in the refrigerator, and roll it out while sipping a Ghia before my guests arrive. And I always make extra—it keeps in the freezer for months and turns a lazy night into a delight.

In this chapter you will find two simple pasta recipes to get you started: a traditional Egg Pasta Dough (page 108) and a vegan Semolina Pasta Dough (page 110). The recipes in this chapter are meant to highlight the delicacy of pasta dough made with your own hands, but store-bought dried pasta will also work just as well if, like me, you sometimes feel a little lazy!

> **PASTA SHAPING NOTE:** Whatever you're making, keep any rolled pasta covered with a damp towel while you work, to save them from drying out.

UNIVERSAL PASTA COOKING NOTES

- When reserving pasta water, scoop from the middle of the pot, not the bottom where semolina flour settles. You want the starchy water that creates silky sauces, not the cloudy sediment.

- If cooking with dried pasta, use a lighter hand with the salt in your cooking water—dried pasta cooks a lot longer and absorbs more salt than fresh.

EGG PASTA DOUGH

MAKES ABOUT 1 POUND OF DOUGH (SERVES 4 TO 6) • **PREP TIME:** 15 MINUTES ACTIVE KNEADING • **COOK TIME:** 2 TO 3 MINUTES • **REST TIME:** 30 MINUTES TO 24 HOURS

Making pasta from scratch sounds ambitious, but the formula is simple and forgiving: 1 egg for every 100 g of flour. The rest is just patience—kneading until the dough is silky smooth, then letting it rest until it feels like velvet. While finely ground "00" flour makes the silkiest pasta, all-purpose works perfectly well. I always have fresh pasta in my freezer, it's my trick to an impromptu but impressive dinner with friends.

See opposite for information on pasta shaping and storing.

300 g "00" or all-purpose flour, plus more as needed

3 eggs

1 teaspoon kosher salt

Semolina flour, for dusting

1. Place the "00" flour on a clean work surface. Make a well in the flour, then crack the eggs into the well and add the salt. Using a fork, gradually incorporate flour from the edges until all the flour is combined with the eggs.

2. Knead the dough with the heel of your hand for about 10 minutes, until the dough becomes smooth and velvety; don't worry if it looks very shaggy for a little while. You don't need a lot of strength, you're just "working" the dough. If it feels too dry, wet your hands slightly and continue kneading. If too sticky, dust with more flour. Trust your hands—they'll tell you when the texture is right. You'll know the dough is ready when it feels like a soft baby's head and bounces back when pressed. Wrap tightly in plastic or a clean damp tea towel and let rest at room temperature for 30 minutes or in the refrigerator for up to 24 hours (for beginners, the dough will be more pliable with a bit more resting time).

3. Lightly flour your work surface with "00" flour. To shape, divide the dough into 6 pieces and shape them into flat discs. Use your hand to flatten a disc of dough into an oblong shape, about 1 inch thick. Dust the top with semolina flour to prevent sticking. Dust a rolling pin with more flour and use it to roll out the dough until it is paper thin. Repeat with all the balls.

4. If using a pasta machine, you can use it to create many shapes, including tagliolini, spaghetti, and large sheets for lasagna.

5. The pasta can be made ahead and refrigerated for up to 2 days or frozen for up to 3 months on semolina-dusted trays.

6. Working in batches to prevent sticking, cook the pasta in well-salted boiling water—fresh pasta takes just 2 to 3 minutes, so it doesn't have much time to absorb the salt. You'll know the pasta is done when it floats to the surface and feels tender but still has a slight bite.

SHAPING AND STORING EGG PASTA DOUGH

Egg pasta dough is moist and silky, best in long strings or sheets that cling to and carry salt and sauce: It's also the best option for fresh lasagna sheets.

- **FOR LINGUINE OR TAGLIOLINI:** Roll the dough thin, then either use your pasta machine's cutting attachment or fold the sheets and slice by hand into ¼-inch strips.
- **FOR PAPPARDELLE:** Cut into generous 1-inch ribbons.
- **FOR LASAGNA SHEETS:** Roll to the second-thinnest setting on your pasta machine and cut into rectangles to fit your baking dish.

TO STORE: Fresh pasta is best used within a couple hours, but life doesn't always cooperate with our pasta-making schedules. For same-day use, keep the shaped pasta refrigerated. If you need to store it longer, dust the shaped pasta lightly with semolina flour, arrange on parchment-lined trays, and cover with plastic wrap—it'll keep in the refrigerator for 2 days. For longer storage, freeze the pasta on semolina-dusted trays until solid (about an hour), then transfer to freezer bags or a storage container. Frozen pasta keeps for 3 months and cooks directly from frozen—just add an extra minute or two to the cooking time.

SEMOLINA PASTA DOUGH

SERVES 4 • **PREP TIME:** 20 MINUTES • **REST TIME:** 1 HOUR • **COOK TIME:** 3 TO 4 MINUTES

While egg pasta gets most of the attention, this simple combination of semolina and water creates something special: a satisfyingly firm and slightly coarse texture that shines in flavorful sauces. It creates the magical moment when sauce and pasta hit your tongue separately but at the same time. Don't be discouraged by how shaggy and stubborn this dough feels at first; it's actually quite forgiving once you work through the initially crumbly stage.

This dough is perfect for small hand-shaped pasta like cavatelli or trofie; keeping the shapes pretty small ensures they maintain that satisfying chew.

2⅓ cups (350 g) semolina flour, plus more for dusting

¾ cup (175 ml) very hot water

1. Place the flour on a clean work surface. Make a well in the flour, then slowly add the hot water into the well. Using a fork, incorporate the flour into the water in a circular motion until you have a thick paste.

2. When the dough becomes too thick for the fork, use your hands to gradually fold in the remaining flour. Don't worry if it looks very shaggy for a little while—just keep kneading for about 10 minutes. Knead the dough vigorously by stretching it forward with the heel of your hand, then folding it halfway over on itself. Do this a few times in one direction, then rotate the dough 90 degrees and repeat, shifting 90 degrees every few strokes. If the dough feels dry and crumbly, wet your hands and continue kneading. If it's too sticky, dust with a little more flour. Trust your hands—they'll tell you when the texture is right. The dough should be smooth and spring back when pressed.

3. Wrap the dough tightly in plastic and let it rest at room temperature for at least 1 hour, up to overnight, before shaping. I find this dough much easier to shape if it rests a little longer.

4. To shape into cavatelli or trofie, see the guide on page 112. This pasta can be frozen for up to 3 months; just drop it in boiling water straight from the freezer.

SHAPING AND STORING SEMOLINA PASTA DOUGH

This dough is perfect for rustic, hand-formed shapes that hold their texture. But be sure to let your dough rest before you begin shaping.

- **FOR CAVATELLI:** Roll small pieces of dough into logs about ½ inch thick, cut into ½-inch pieces, then use your thumb to drag each piece across the work surface (use a gnocchi board if you have one) to create shell shapes.
- **FOR TROFIE:** Cut the dough into 4 pieces. One at a time, leaving the other pieces covered, roll each piece of dough into a rope about ½ inch thick on a lightly floured work surface. Next, cut into large pea-size pieces.
- Take each pea-size piece and roll it with light pressure, holding your hand at a slight angle so that it twists into a thin log.

With the outer edge of your palm and with light pressure, roll the log down with your hand at a 45-degree angle so the dough twists into a spiral. Each piece should look like a little pigtail about 1 inch long and feel firm but springy. If your trofie stick while shaping, dust with semolina flour. Don't worry if your first few look irregular—they will taste just as good and you'll get the hang of it.

TO STORE For same-day use, dust with semolina flour and keep at room temperature for up to 4 hours—I prefer this to chilling it in the refrigerator, to prevent it from getting too firm. For longer storage, freeze the shaped pasta on semolina-dusted trays until solid (about 1 hour), then transfer to freezer bags. It keeps beautifully for 6 months and cooks directly from frozen—just add an extra minute to the cooking time.

GREEN LASAGNA AS IN PORTOFINO

SERVES 6 TO 8 • **PREP TIME:** 1 HOUR • **COOK TIME:** 45 MINUTES

This specific lasagna is typically Ligurian; I discovered it at a little restaurant by the beach in Portofino and it's been one of my favorites ever since. The layers of pasta turn vibrant green with pesto instead of the usual tomato sauce. While it's a project when made entirely from scratch, it's delicious using store-bought pasta sheets or sauce.

4 cups (1 L) whole milk

½ stick (60 g) butter, plus more for greasing

¼ cup (60 g) flour

Pinch of freshly grated nutmeg

Kosher salt and freshly ground black pepper

6 fresh lasagna sheets (from Egg Pasta Dough, page 108) or store-bought dried

2 batches Pistou (page 94)

1 cup (100 g) freshly grated Parmesan

1. To make the béchamel, in a small saucepan heat the milk over medium heat until steaming and bubbles form around the edges, but don't let it boil. In a large saucepan over medium heat, melt the butter. Add the flour and whisk constantly until the roux is golden and fragrant, about 2 minutes. Gradually whisk in the hot milk. Simmer, stirring often, until the béchamel is thick enough to coat the back of a spoon. Stir in the nutmeg and season with salt and pepper.

2. Preheat the oven to 350°F. Bring a large pot of salted water to a boil (see page 106).

3. If using fresh pasta, refer to page 109 to make the lasagna sheets, then cut them into rectangles to fit a 9 × 13-inch baking dish. Working one at a time, boil the sheets for about 1 minute each. Transfer to clean kitchen towels to drain.

4. If using dried pasta, cook several sheets at a time until just tender (check the package instructions, usually 8 to 9 minutes). Transfer to clean kitchen towels to drain.

5. To assemble, butter a 9 × 13-inch baking dish. Spread about ½ cup béchamel at the bottom of the dish (you need a bit more béchamel here than in the other layers). Add a layer of pasta, then spread about ⅓ cup of béchamel, followed by ¼ cup pistou and a sprinkle of Parmesan. Repeat these layers until you run out of ingredients (usually 4 or 5 layers; the sixth sheet is for insurance). Finish with the béchamel and a generous amount of Parmesan, going all the way to the corners of the dish to make crispy edges worth fighting over.

6. Cover the pan with foil and bake for 30 minutes. Uncover and bake 15 minutes more, until golden and bubbling.

7. Let rest for 10 minutes before serving—this lasagna is rather loose, so it'll be easier to cut but still plenty hot. Leftovers can be covered and refrigerated for up to 3 days, or frozen for up to 3 months. Reheat in the oven until warmed through.

LINGUINE WITH CLAMS AND CHILE

SERVES 4 TO 6 • **PREP TIME:** 15 MINUTES • **COOK TIME:** 10 MINUTES (WITH FRESH PASTA) OR 15 MINUTES (WITH DRIED)

A bowl of steaming pasta with clams reminds me instantly of seaside restaurants on the Riviera. While the dish is traditionally made with spaghetti, I love using freshly cut linguine here—the delicate strands drink up the briny sauce in a way dried pasta never quite manages. Let the clams open slowly, adding their salty goodness to the garlic, chile, and olive oil.

See page 109 for information on pasta shaping and storing.

Kosher salt

¼ cup (60 ml) olive oil

6 garlic cloves, very thinly sliced

1 whole fresh red chile, such as Fresno or serrano, seeded and sliced paper-thin, or 1 teaspoon red pepper flakes

2 pounds (900 g) littleneck clams, scrubbed

½ cup (120 ml) dry white wine (I like Sauvignon Blanc)

½ cup (25 g) parsley leaves, roughly chopped

1 pound (450 g) fresh linguine (from Egg Pasta Dough, page 108) or store-bought dried

Freshly ground black pepper to taste

Your best olive oil, for drizzling

1. Make sure all the ingredients are prepped and ready to go—this dish comes together quickly.

2. Bring a large pot of salted water to boil and salt it generously (see page 106). If you're using fresh pasta, hold off on cooking it until the clams are almost ready. If using dried pasta, add it when the water comes to a boil and cook for about 8 minutes.

3. In a large saucepan, heat the olive oil over medium heat. Add the garlic and chile, letting them sizzle gently until fragrant but not browned, about 2 minutes. Add the clams and wine, cover the pan, and cook until the clams release their juices and open up, 5 to 7 minutes. Discard any clams that did not open.

4. If using fresh pasta, add it now and cook until it is just tender but still has some bite, 2 to 3 minutes. Carefully ladle out and reserve 1 cup of the starchy pasta water (see the guide on page 106). Drain the pasta.

5. Add the pasta to the clam pan, along with enough of the reserved pasta water to create a glossy sauce—you may not need the whole cup. Use tongs to toss everything together until the sauce turns silky and coats each strand of pasta. Finish with the parsley, season with black pepper, and top with a drizzle of your best olive oil. Leftovers can be covered and refrigerated for up to 4 days, or frozen for up to 3 months. Reheat in the oven until warmed through.

PASTA AL LIMONE

SERVES 4 TO 6 • **PREP TIME:** 10 MINUTES • **COOK TIME:** 10 MINUTES (WITH FRESH PASTA) OR 15 MINUTES (WITH DRIED)

This is a bright, silky tangle of pasta that's all about good lemons. While the traditional version relies solely on butter and starchy pasta water for its sauce, I like to add a splash of cream for extra richness. The key is using unwaxed organic lemons since the zest is crucial here. Make this with fresh Egg Pasta Dough and it becomes restaurant-worthy as the delicate noodles drink up the lemony sauce.

See page 109 for information on pasta shaping and storing.

Kosher salt

2 or 3 organic lemons

½ stick (60 g) butter

1 tablespoon olive oil

¼ cup (60 ml) heavy cream

12 ounces fresh tagliolini or spaghetti (from Egg Pasta Dough, page 108) or store-bought dried

½ cup (50 g) freshly grated Parmesan or pecorino, plus more for serving

Freshly ground black pepper

1. Bring a large pot of salted water to boil and salt it generously—it should taste like the sea (see page 106). Finely zest both lemons (you want just the yellow zest, not the white pith), then juice them.

2. In a large sauté pan, melt the butter with the oil over medium heat. Add the lemon zest and cook until fragrant, about 1 minute. Add the juice and let it sizzle briefly. Stir in the cream and lower the heat to keep warm.

3. Start cooking the pasta now. Carefully ladle out and reserve 1 cup of the starchy pasta water (see the guide on page 106). Drain the pasta.

4. Add the pasta to the lemon sauce, using tongs to toss vigorously. Add the cheese and enough of the reserved pasta water to create a glossy sauce that clings to every strand—you may not need the whole cup. Toss to incorporate the cheese and season with pepper. Serve immediately with more cheese alongside.

GREEN TROFIE

PÂTES AU PISTOU COMME EN LIGURIE

SERVES 4 TO 6 • **PREP TIME:** 45 MINUTES • **COOK TIME:** 3 MINUTES

While most recipes in this book were passed down to me, this one is my own addition to our family's repertoire. I've fallen in love with trofie, these little twisted pasta shapes from Liguria that seem designed to catch every bit of herb sauce. Shaping them takes practice, but there's something meditative about rolling each piece into a twist. And don't worry too much about perfection—once they're coated in pesto, they all look beautiful.

See page 112 for information on pasta shaping and storing.

1 pound (450 g) fresh trofie (from Semolina Pasta Dough, page 110)

Kosher salt

3 tablespoons butter

1 batch Pistou (page 94)

⅔ cup (60 g) freshly grated Parmesan, plus more for serving

Your best olive oil, for drizzling

Toasted pine nuts, for garnish

1. Bring a large pot of salted water to a boil. Add the trofie and cook until they float to the surface, about 3 minutes. Carefully ladle out and reserve 1 cup of the starchy pasta water (see the guide on page 106). Drain the pasta.

2. In a large saucepan, melt the butter over medium heat. Add the pistou and a splash of the reserved pasta water, then add the hot pasta and toss, spooning in more pasta water as needed until the sauce turns silky and clings to each twist. The trofie should look wet, in the best way! Divide among bowls and finish with the Parmesan, a drizzle of your best olive oil, and a handful of toasted pine nuts.

CAVATELLI WITH SAUSAGE AND POMODORO

SERVES 4 • **PREP TIME:** 15 MINUTES • **COOK TIME:** 30 MINUTES

This is the kind of dish that makes you grateful for a well-stocked kitchen. If you keep good Italian sausages in the freezer and have some pasta on hand, you're most of the way there—this whole dish comes together in the time it takes to boil the pasta water. While any pasta shape will work, this is particularly good with cavatelli—their little grooves catch every bit of sauce.

¼ cup (60 ml) olive oil

2 garlic cloves, crushed

1 pound (450 g) Italian sausage, casings removed

1 pound (450 g) ripe tomatoes, peeled and roughly chopped

2 bay leaves

Kosher salt

1 pound (450 g) fresh cavatelli (from Semolina Pasta Dough, page 110) or store-bought dried

⅔ cup (150 ml) dry white wine (I like a Pinot Grigio or Sauvignon Blanc)

Pecorino cheese, for serving

Red pepper flakes, for serving

1. Heat the olive oil in a large pot over medium-low heat. Add the garlic and gently fry it until fragrant, about 2 minutes (take care not to burn it).

2. Add the sausage, breaking it up with a spoon into crumbles. Cook until no pink remains and the sausage starts to brown slightly, about 8 minutes. Add the wine and let it bubble and reduce for about 2 minutes.

3. Add the tomatoes and bay leaves to the pot and simmer until the sauce thickens and becomes almost creamy, about 10 minutes. Season with 2 teaspoons kosher salt.

4. Bring a large pot of salted water to a boil, making it as salty as the sea (see page 106). Add the cavatelli and cook until almost done, with a minute or two left to cook. Use a slotted spoon to transfer the cavatelli to the sauce, letting some of the pasta water come along as its starch will nicely bind the sauce to the pasta. Reserve 1 cup of the starchy pasta water (see the guide on page 106). Simmer for a minute or two, stirring slowly, until the pasta is cooked and the sauce clings to each piece.

5. Serve hot, passing around grated pecorino and red pepper flakes for those who want a little heat. Leftovers can be covered and refrigerated for up to 4 days, or frozen for up to 3 months. Reheat in the oven until warmed through.

> **NOTE:** *If making this dish when tomatoes are not at their peak, a tablespoon of tomato paste helps sweeten the sauce. Add it to the pan when you add the sausage.*

GNOCCHI WITH CONFIT CHERRY TOMATOES

SERVES 4 TO 6 • **PREP TIME:** 1 HOUR • **COOK TIME:** 5 MINUTES

These gnocchi are my little sister Manon's favorite treats. Making gnocchi is a meditation in patience—each little pillow of potato pasta shaped by hand. The key is getting the potatoes as fluffy as possible: Bake them until very tender, then rice them while they're still piping hot. I love serving them with slow-roasted cherry tomatoes, which collapse into a rich sauce.

2 pounds (900 g) russet potatoes, scrubbed

Kosher salt

1½ cups (180 g) all-purpose flour, plus more for the work surface

1 batch Confit Cherry Tomatoes (page 9)

3 garlic cloves, sliced

¼ cup (60 ml) olive oil

Fresh basil leaves, for garnish

Flaky salt

1. Preheat the oven to 400°F.

2. Pierce the potatoes several times with a fork and bake them until very tender, about 1 hour. While still hot, carefully cut them in half and, working quickly, scoop out the flesh and pass it through a ricer onto a cutting board—the heat helps keep them light and fluffy.

3. Sprinkle the potatoes with 1 teaspoon kosher salt and about half the flour. Gently gather everything into a dough, adding more flour only as needed to prevent sticking. You want the dough to feel soft and pliant, slightly tacky, and shaggy. Stop working as soon as the dough comes together and isn't too sticky.

4. Lightly flour a work surface, then roll out the dough into ropes about ½ inch thick. Using a bench scraper or pastry cutter with clean,

decisive strokes, cut the ropes into 1-inch pieces. (You can also roll each piece on a gnocchi board or the back of a fork to make ridges.) Spread out the gnocchi on the work surface and let them air-dry for 30 minutes.

5. While the gnocchi are resting, bring a large pot of well-salted water to a boil.

6. Meanwhile, in a medium saucepan over medium heat, gently warm the tomatoes, garlic, and olive oil until the garlic is fragrant, about 3 minutes.

7. Working in batches, cook the gnocchi in the boiling water until they float, about 3 minutes.

8. With a slotted spoon, transfer them to the tomatoes in the pan and toss gently. Tear some basil leaves on top, then finish with flaky salt and enjoy immediately. Leftovers can be covered and refrigerated for up to 4 days, or frozen for up to 3 months. Reheat in the oven until warmed through.

NOTE: *Uncooked gnocchi freeze on a flour-dusted tray. Once frozen, transfer them to a freezer bag and store in the freezer for up to 6 months. Cook them straight from frozen, adding about 1 minute to the cooking time.*

RICOTTA GNUDI WITH SAGE BUTTER

SERVES 4 • **PREP TIME:** 20 MINUTES • **COOK TIME:** 10 MINUTES

Sometimes the humblest dishes are the most impressive. These are cloud-like dumplings made from little more than ricotta and flour. The trick is using well-drained ricotta—the drier it is, the less flour you'll need and the lighter your gnudi will be.

16 ounces (450 g) whole milk ricotta

½ cup (60 g) all-purpose flour, plus more for rolling

Kosher salt

1 stick (113 g) butter

2 tablespoons olive oil

12 sage leaves

Freshly ground black pepper to taste

Freshly grated Parmesan, for serving

1. In a fine-mesh sieve set over a small bowl, drain the ricotta for at least 30 minutes (you can discard the whey in the bowl, or use it as a high-protein liquid in soups, pancakes, and smoothies). Transfer the drained ricotta to a medium bowl and add the flour and a pinch of salt. Mix until just combined—the gnudi dough will be soft and slightly sticky.

2. With floured hands, roll the gnudi into balls just slightly bigger than unshelled walnuts (about 1½ inches in diameter). As you shape the gnudi, place them on a rimmed sheet pan dusted with flour. Transfer the gnudi to the refrigerator and chill until ready to cook.

3. Bring a large pot of salted water to a gentle boil.

4. Meanwhile, start the sauce. In a small, wide sauté pan over medium-low heat, combine the butter and olive oil. When the butter has melted, add the sage leaves. Let the butter bubble gently—you'll see the milk solids start to turn golden and sink to the bottom, the sage will crisp up, and the whole thing will smell wonderfully nutty, 3 to 4 minutes. Lower the heat if the butter starts to sputter or the sage begins to crisp too quickly—brown butter is an easy sauce to make, but you have to keep your eyes on it because it goes from golden to burned quite quickly. Turn off the heat and set aside until the gnudi are ready.

5. When the water comes to a boil, working in batches, drop in the gnudi and cook until they float to the surface, about 3 minutes. Use a slotted spoon to transfer them directly into the pan with the brown butter and cover them with sauce.

6. Season with pepper and serve the gnudi hot with plenty of Parmesan and the sage leaves arranged on top.

> **NOTE:** *Freeze uncooked gnudi on a flour-dusted tray. Transfer them to a freezer bag and freeze for up to 6 months. Cook them straight from frozen, adding about 1 minute to the cooking time.*

MYMO'S PASTA GRATIN

SERVES 4 TO 6 • **PREP TIME:** 15 MINUTES • **COOK TIME:** 20 MINUTES

This is my family's most cherished recipe, my grandmother's signature gratin de pâtes. It embodies everything I learned from her about cooking—how to make something extraordinary from simple ingredients—and how to never waste a thing. Every bite is magic, but the crispy corners were always fought over at our family table.

3 cups (750 ml) chicken bone broth, homemade (see page 6) or 2 chicken bouillon cubes dissolved in 3 cups water

1 pound (450 g) dried short pasta, such as cavatappi or macaroni

8 ounces (225 g) Gruyère, Comté, or Emmental

4 thick slices day-old bread

8 tablespoons butter, plus more for greasing

Leaves from 4 thyme sprigs

2 teaspoons freshly ground black pepper

Fresh herbs (optional, but I love to use the leaves of a few sprigs of thyme)

1. Preheat the oven to 400°F.

2. In a medium saucepan, bring the broth to a boil. Add the pasta and cook for about 3 minutes less than package instructions— you want it very al dente. The liquid should just cover the pasta by about 1 inch to keep it starchy and very flavorful. This is the key to this recipe!

3. Meanwhile, grate the cheese on the medium holes of a box grater. In a food processor, pulse the bread into coarse crumbs, about ⅛ to ¼ inch. (If the bread is not quite stale, toast it and cool it before processing it.)

4. Butter a large baking dish—round and oval are prettier, but rectangular will give you crispy corners. Dot 2 tablespoons of butter over the bottom, followed by one-third of the bread crumbs, then one-third of the cheese.

5. Using a slotted spoon, transfer the pasta to the dish (reserving the cooking liquid). Add 3 tablespoons of the butter, the thyme leaves, and the pepper and toss gently to combine. Scatter half of the remaining cheese throughout. Pour in enough cooking liquid to come up about two-thirds of the way up the dish (this amount of liquid is what makes it creamy and silky as it bakes).

6. Top generously with the remaining cheese and remaining 3 tablespoons butter and finish with the remaining bread crumbs and herbs (if using).

7. Bake for 15 to 20 minutes, until golden and bubbling. Let rest for 5 minutes before serving to allow the liquid to settle. Leftovers can be covered and refrigerated for up to 4 days. Reheat in the oven until warmed through.

MAINS

A rare picture with my mom, as she was always the one taking the photos. I remember this day vividly.

Running around the kitchen at Christmas dinner in Cannes.

POLPETTES IN LEMONY BRODO

SERVES 4 TO 6 • **PREP TIME:** 15 MINUTES • **COOK TIME:** 35 MINUTES

These are tender little meatballs swimming in a lemony broth—the kind of thing that makes you feel instantly better, no matter the weather. I use beef and veal to make mine, but any combination of meats works well (the fattier the cut, the juicier the meatball). Make a double batch—they freeze really well and make the best emergency dinner with just some broth and whatever greens need using.

FOR THE POLPETTES

½ **pound (225 g) ground beef**

½ **pound (225 g) ground veal**

1 cup (100 g) bread crumbs (made from stale bread)

1 egg

1 cup (100 g) freshly grated Parmesan

2 garlic cloves, grated

Handful of parsley, chopped

1 teaspoon kosher salt

Freshly ground black pepper

3 tablespoons olive oil

FOR THE BRODO

6 cups (1.4 L) chicken broth, homemade (see page 6), or store-bought

2 bay leaves

1 lemon, juiced

1 cup (180 g) orzo

2 handfuls (50 g) of spinach or other greens

FOR SERVING

1 lemon, cut into wedges

Freshly ground black pepper

Your best olive oil

1. **PREPARE THE POLPETTES:** In a large bowl, mix the meats, bread crumbs, egg, Parmesan, garlic, parsley, and the salt until combined. Form into balls that are just smaller than a golf ball (you'll have about 20 balls).

2. **PREPARE THE BRODO:** In a large stockpot or other heavy pot, heat the olive oil on medium heat. Brown the meatballs on all sides until golden, about 5 minutes total. Add the broth, bay leaves, and lemon juice. Simmer gently for 8 minutes. Add the orzo and cook until tender, about 7 minutes. Add the greens and simmer until just wilted.

3. **TO SERVE:** Plate the polpettes in shallow bowls and ladle the brodo over them. Grind some pepper on top and drizzle in your best olive oil. Serve with lemon wedges.

> **NOTE:** *Polpettes freeze easily—just freeze the raw meatballs on a tray, then transfer to a freezer bag. They will keep in the freezer for up to 3 months. Thaw overnight if you like them well browned or take a shortcut and cook straight from frozen, adding a few extra minutes to the simmering time.*

BROCHETTES

SERVES 4 (ABOUT 8 SKEWERS) • **PREP TIME:** 15 MINUTES PLUS 30 MINUTES TO 4 HOURS
MARINATING • **COOK TIME:** 10 MINUTES

These are the skewers I make all summer long—chunks of good lamb or beef interspersed with any vegetables. For tender, juicy results, look for cuts with some fat marbled throughout: Lamb shoulder is perfect, or try well-marbled beef sirloin. If you can find only leaner cuts, just watch them carefully on the grill—they'll cook faster. Cherry tomatoes are a nice addition if you have them on hand: They blister and burst, creating little pockets of sauce right on the skewer.

2 pounds (900 g) lamb shoulder or beef sirloin

3 tablespoons olive oil, plus more for brushing

4 garlic cloves, smashed

2 rosemary sprigs

Generous pinch of kosher salt

2 yellow onions

Flaky salt and freshly ground black pepper to taste

1. Cut the meat into 1½-inch cubes—any smaller and they'll overcook. Place them in a large bowl and toss with the oil, garlic, rosemary, and kosher salt. Let marinate at room temperature for 30 minutes (or refrigerate for up to 4 hours, bringing back to room temperature before grilling).

2. Cut the onions into 1½-inch chunks. Thread onto metal or wooden skewers (see Note), alternating the meat and vegetables. Leave a little space between the pieces so everything cooks evenly.

3. Heat a grill or grill pan on high until very hot. Brush the meat and veggie skewers with oil and season them with flaky salt and pepper. Grill 3 to 4 minutes per side for medium-rare, turning only once.

> **NOTE:** If using wooden skewers, soak them in water for 30 minutes before using. Plan on two skewers per person as a main course.

MAKE IT YOUR OWN

Try adding peppers, cherry tomatoes, and/or any vegetables you have on hand that don't require too much cooking and can handle the grill flame.

WHOLE BRANZINO

SERVES 4 • **PREP TIME:** 30 MINUTES • **COOK TIME:** 15 MINUTES

Don't let cooking a whole fish intimidate you—it's one of the most forgiving methods there is. The bones protect the flesh from overheating while it cooks, keeping it moist. And there's something celebratory about bringing a whole fish to the table, especially when it's dripping with Put-on-Everything Green Sauce, a catchall term for a loose adaptation of chimichurri that I like to slather on every meat and fish when hosting.

2 whole branzini or other whole fish (about 1 pound / 450 g each), cleaned (see Note)

1 lemon, thinly sliced

A few rosemary sprigs

Olive oil

Flaky salt

Freshly ground black pepper

Put-on-Everything Green Sauce (recipe follows), for serving

1 lemon, cut into wedges, for serving

1. Preheat the oven to 400°F.

2. Pat the fish very dry—this is crucial for crispy skin. Using a sharp knife, make three diagonal slits on each side of the fish, cutting through the skin and about ½ inch into the flesh at a 45-degree angle. Season generously inside and out with flaky salt, pushing some into the slits. Stuff the cavities with lemon slices and rosemary sprigs.

3. Rub both sides of the fish with oil and place the fish on a large sheet pan. Roast until just cooked through, about 15 minutes. The flesh should be opaque and flake easily when tested with a fork at the thickest part. For extra-crispy skin, finish under the broiler for 2 to 3 minutes.

4. To fillet and serve each fish, remove the aromatics from inside the cavities and discard. Run a sharp knife along the backbone of the fish. Gently lift the top fillet away from the bones. The hardest part is done! The backbone can now be lifted out in one piece, leaving the bottom fillet intact. Serve one fillet to each person, then scoop out the fish cheeks with a little fork and give them to your favorite guest.

5. Serve with olive oil or Put-on-Everything Green Sauce and lemon wedges.

> **NOTE:** *While branzino is a favorite for being tender, any whole fish works here—remember to adjust the cooking time based on size (about 10 minutes per inch of thickness).*

PUT-ON-EVERYTHING GREEN SAUCE

LOOSE CHIMICHURRI

MAKES 1 CUP • **PREP TIME:** 15 MINUTES

This sauce makes everything better—fish, vegetables, bread, even a soft-boiled egg. The recipe is also infinitely forgiving: Use whatever herbs are about to wilt, the last spoonful of tapenade, that handful of olives at the bottom of the jar. The key is building layers of flavor—bright herbs, punchy garlic, and good olive oil, tasting as you go until everything's in balance.

4 garlic cloves, minced

Zest and juice of 2 lemons

1 teaspoon kosher salt, plus more to taste

½ teaspoon freshly ground black pepper, plus more to taste

2 cups mixed soft herbs, such as parsley, cilantro, and mint

1 small fresh red chile, or 1 teaspoon red pepper flakes

½ cup (120 ml) your best olive oil

2 tablespoons capers, drained, or chopped olives (optional)

1. In a medium bowl, combine the garlic, lemon zest and juice, salt, and pepper. Let this sit while you chop the herbs—it takes the bite out of the garlic.

2. Wash and dry the herbs well. For the parsley, pick the leaves from the stems, but don't worry about the cilantro—the stems are delicious and can be chopped right in. Roughly chop everything—no need to be too precious about it. I actually prefer the herbs when they're a bit rustic, especially if I'm serving this with meat.

3. Add the chopped herbs, red pepper flakes, olive oil, and the capers (if using) to the bowl with the garlic mixture. The sauce should be loose enough to spoon easily but not swimming in oil. Taste and adjust—it should make your mouth water and be just a little salty at the end. Use this sauce immediately or cover and store it in the refrigerator for up to 3 days. Bring to room temperature and stir well before using.

POISSON EN PAPILLOTE

FISH IN PARCHMENT PAPER

SERVES 4 • **PREP TIME:** 15 MINUTES • **COOK TIME:** 10 TO 15 MINUTES

Cooking *en papillote* (in parchment) is one of those techniques that sounds fancy but is actually foolproof. The paper packet creates a perfect little steam chamber, infusing the fish with whatever herbs and aromatics you tuck inside. My favorite part is bringing the puffed packets to the table, letting each person unwrap their own bundle of fragrant steam. I love adding odds and ends of vegetables to use up—thin ribbons of fennel, cherry tomatoes about to burst, the last few sprigs of herbs.

FOR EACH PACKET

Handful of mixed vegetables, such as cherry tomatoes, sliced fennel, and zucchini ribbons

One 6-ounce (170 g) salmon, snapper, or any whitefish fillet, such as cod

2 thyme sprigs

1 rosemary sprig

1 bay leaf

1 tablespoon salted butter

1 tablespoon your best olive oil

Splash of white wine (optional)

1 lemon

Flaky salt and freshly ground black pepper to taste

A scoop of miso paste, if using cod (optional)

1. Preheat the oven to 425°F. Cut four 12 × 16-inch hearts from parchment paper and fold them in half lengthwise.

2. To make a packet, on one side of each heart, near the crease, arrange the vegetables. Place the fish on top, then the herbs, butter, olive oil, wine (if using), and the lemon. Season well with salt and pepper.

3. Fold the paper over the ingredients and crimp the edges tightly, starting from the pointed end and working your way up to create a sealed packet. Place the packet on a sheet pan. Repeat to make the other packets.

4. Bake 8 to 10 minutes for thin fillets, 12 to 15 minutes for thicker ones. The packets should puff up like balloons. If for whatever reason the steam escapes, the juices of the veggies will keep everything moist. Not to worry—this one truly is impossible to mess up.

5. Serve the papillotes directly on plates, letting each person open their own packet at the table. Part of the joy is that first waft of herb-scented steam. The fish will come out incredibly fragrant and tender, with yummy juices to be scooped up from the bottom of the papillote.

> **NOTE:** *The vegetables should be sliced very thin so they cook in the same time as the fish. The wine is lovely but not mandatory—it adds flavor to the steam that makes everything tender.*

CHICKEN WITH FORTY CLOVES OF GARLIC

SERVES 4 TO 6 • **PREP TIME:** 15 MINUTES • **COOK TIME:** 2 HOURS

A roast chicken might be my ultimate comfort food—I can never resist picking at the crispy skin or soaking bread in the garlicky jus. While forty cloves may sound excessive, the garlic mellows and sweetens as it cooks, turning into a soft, spreadable condiment. This is my Sunday version, when I have all the time to cook it low and slow until the meat nearly falls off the bone. Stuffing the chicken with a Cured Lemon adds a burst of flavor and moisture from the inside, and if you prefer to make this into a full meal, lay a bed of vegetables underneath the chicken.

1 large chicken (about 4 pounds / 1.8 kg), giblets removed

Kosher salt and freshly ground black pepper

A few thyme sprigs

A few rosemary sprigs

1 bay leaf

1 Cured Lemon (page 10) or fresh lemon

2 shallots, halved

Small root vegetables, such as carrots, onions, and potatoes (optional)

Olive oil

40 garlic cloves (from about 3 heads), unpeeled

½ stick (60 g) cold salted butter

2 garlic cloves, minced

1. If you have time, several hours before cooking, pat the chicken very dry with paper towels and leave uncovered in the refrigerator—this helps the skin crisp. Bring to room temperature before cooking.

2. Preheat the oven to 325°F.

3. Season the chicken generously inside and out with salt and pepper. Stuff the cavity with the herbs, the whole cured or fresh lemon, and the shallots.

4. If using the vegetables, toss them with olive oil and arrange them in the roasting pan. Place the unpeeled garlic cloves on top (or directly in the pan if you're not using vegetables). Rub the chicken all over with the cold butter, minced garlic, and more salt and pepper, getting under the skin where possible. Place the chicken breast side up on the garlic and vegetables and drizzle with oil again. A unique texture and flavor comes from mixing butter and olive oil.

5. Roast low and slow, about 2 hours, basting occasionally with the pan juices. For extra-golden skin, remove the pan, transfer any vegetables to a bowl (they'll have soaked up plenty of chicken fat by now), and return the chicken to the oven at 425°F for the final 10 minutes.

Continues

6. The chicken is ready when the legs wiggle loose and the juices run clear.

7. Let the chicken rest 15 minutes before carving. While it rests, tip the roasting pan and check your jus—if it's too reduced, add a splash of water; if it's too thin, let it bubble on the stovetop for a few minutes. Spoon off any excess fat, but save all those golden drippings.

8. To carve, first remove the legs, then the wings. For the breast meat, find the breastbone and cut down each side, following the ribs. Don't worry about being too neat and don't throw away the carcass without getting every last morsel—those bits soaked in jus are often the best part of the meal. Serve with the garlic and vegetables (if using) on the side.

> **NOTE:** *The cured lemon helps keep the meat moist from the inside while the butter creates that golden, crispy skin. If you choose to roast the chicken over vegetables, the vegetables will cook in the delicious chicken fat—just remember to rescue them before a final high-heat blast.*

DAUBE PROVENÇALE

SERVES 6 • **PREP TIME:** 30 MINUTES PLUS OVERNIGHT MARINATING • **COOK TIME:** 3 HOURS

Think of this as Provence's answer to boeuf bourguignon—a wine-braised beef enriched with orange zest and olives instead of bacon and mushrooms. The combination of the velvety sauce, the meat, and the zest of the orange is surprising in the best, subtlest way. Like its northern cousin, it demands patience: proper browning, slow cooking until the meat nearly melts, and ideally a day's rest for the flavors to deepen. Since the wine is the backbone of this dish, use a good-quality, full-bodied red that you'd be happy to drink.

3 pounds (1.4 kg) chuck roast, cut into 2-inch cubes

1 bottle (750 ml) full-bodied red wine (I like Cabernet Sauvignon, Syrah, or Côte du Rhône)

4 shallots, halved or quartered

4 carrots, cut into 2-inch chunks

2 celery stalks, diced

10 garlic cloves, smashed

2 oranges, peeled and cut into ½-inch strips

6 thyme sprigs

2 rosemary sprigs

3 bay leaves

2 whole cloves

1 star anise

2 yellow onions, quartered

3 tablespoons flour

¼ cup (60 ml) olive oil, plus more as needed

20 pearl onions

2 teaspoons sugar

2 tablespoons tomato paste

2 tablespoons anchovy paste

2 cups (250 ml) beef broth, homemade (page 6) or store-bought, plus more as needed

1 cup (140 g) pitted Niçoise or Taggiasca olives

Kosher salt

Freshly ground black pepper

Cooked wide egg noodles or fresh pasta and freshly chopped parsley, for serving

1. The night before: In a large Dutch oven or other heavy pot with a lid, combine the meat with half of the wine, the shallots, carrots, celery, garlic, orange peel, herbs, and spices. Cover and refrigerate overnight.

2. The next day: Drain the meat and vegetables, reserving the marinade. Pat the meat very dry with paper towels—this is crucial for a good crust. Dust lightly with the flour. Heat the olive oil in the same Dutch oven over medium-high heat. In batches, lay the meat in a single layer to brown. Don't touch it until it is deeply crusty underneath (about 8 minutes per batch). Set aside.

Continues

3. In a large bowl, prepare an ice water bath. Bring a small pot of water to a boil on medium-high heat. Drop in the pearl onions for 2 minutes, then remove with a slotted spoon and transfer to the ice water bath to stop the cooking. Once they're cool enough to handle, peel off the skins—they should slip off easily.

4. Add the pearl onions to the Dutch oven, sprinkle with the sugar, and cook until caramelized, stirring occasionally, about 5 minutes. Add the reserved vegetables and cook until just softened, stirring occasionally, about 5 minutes. Stir in the tomato paste and anchovy paste until fragrant. The anchovy paste adds a lot of depth of flavor, and I promise it will not make your dish taste like anchovy.

5. Preheat the oven to 325°F.

6. Return the meat to the pot and add the remaining half-bottle wine, reserved marinade, and broth. Bring to a gentle simmer on the stove, then cover and cook in the oven for 3 hours, until the meat falls apart, stirring every 30 minutes or so and scraping the bits of marinade off the sides of the pot and into the sauce. When the meat is almost done and you'll be cooking for about 30 minutes more, add the olives. The finished sauce should coat a spoon—if too thin, uncover the pot and simmer it on the stovetop; if too thick, add a splash of broth. Season with salt and pepper.

7. Serve over pasta and scatter with parsley.

> **NOTE:** *Like all braises, this dish improves overnight. Make it a day ahead if you can and reheat it on the stove. And don't skip drying the meat—you want the pieces to be nicely browned, not sadly boiled chunks.*
>
> *Make the pasta yourself! See the recipe for egg pasta dough on page 108.*

RÔTI DE PÉPÉ

MY GRANDFATHER'S ROAST BEEF

SERVES 6 • **PREP TIME:** 15 MINUTES • **COOK TIME:** 40 MINUTES

This is my grandfather's signature Sunday roast beef—what the French call rôti parisien—a rather effortless dish that only needs good meat, plenty of butter, and a heavy pan. Twenty minutes of cooking per kilo (2.2 pounds) is the magic number—any longer and you'll lose that rosy center. While you reduce the pan drippings into a jus, the meat must rest a full 15 minutes under foil to let the juices distribute all the way to the heart of the roast beef for the most tender texture. Ideally, ask your butcher to tie lardo around it to save you from basting.

One 3-pound (1.3 kg) beef roast (top round or eye of round), tied if needed

Kosher salt and freshly ground black pepper

6 tablespoons unsalted butter

4 thyme sprigs

4 garlic cloves, unpeeled

1. Let the meat come to room temperature, then season it generously with salt and pepper.

2. Preheat the oven to 400°F.

3. In a large Dutch oven or oven-safe sauté pan, melt the butter over medium heat. Brown the meat on all sides until crusty, 8 to 10 minutes total. Add the thyme and garlic.

4. Transfer the beef to the oven. Roast about 30 minutes, basting every 10 minutes or so. Rest a good 15 minutes before serving to let all the juices distribute evenly.

5. Meanwhile, reduce the pan juices over low heat into a nice dense jus. Slice the meat thinly against the grain and serve with the jus.

> **NOTE:** *Cooking garlic like this is called "ail en chemise," or "garlic in its shirt," and this makes the garlic very sweet and like a condiment or a quick confit. My grandfather would spread it on the rôti.*

PETITS FARCIS NIÇOIS

STUFFED VEGETABLES LIKE THEY MAKE IN NICE

SERVES 4 TO 6 (2 OR 3 PIECES PER PERSON) • **PREP TIME:** 15 MINUTES • **COOK TIME:** 45 MINUTES

These delectable stuffed vegetables are probably the first thing I eat when I arrive in Nice—at Chez Davia, preferably! The recipe holds up to many variations—my mother loves to add rice to the stuffing and uses only tomatoes, the rice soaking up all their sweet juices in the oven. I use a mixture of pork and veal for the juiciest filling, though any high-quality ground meat will work splendidly.

4 medium ripe tomatoes, any variety, 3 to 4 inches in diameter

2 onions, any variety

2 medium zucchini, round or long

2 small eggplants, round or long

½ pound (225 g) ground pork

½ pound (225 g) ground veal (or use all pork)

3 garlic cloves, finely minced

½ cup (30 g) fresh bread crumbs, any variety (see Note)

¼ cup (25 g) freshly grated Parmesan

¼ cup (15 g) finely chopped flat-leaf parsley

Olive oil

1 cup (200 g) cooked white or basmati rice (optional)

Kosher salt and freshly ground black pepper

1. Preheat the oven to 375°F.

2. Cut a "hat" off the top of the tomatoes and onions (about ¼ inch from the top). If your zucchini and eggplants are round, cut off the stem end for the hat, then cut a slice from the bottom so they sit flat. For longer vegetables, cut a small slice lengthwise off one side. Carefully hollow out the vegetables using a paring knife or sharp spoon, leaving sturdy shells (leave a couple outside onion layers). Chop the removed flesh and reserve it in a large bowl. Reserve the hats.

3. Add the raw meats, garlic, bread crumbs, Parmesan, parsley, and 2 tablespoons olive oil, and cooked rice (if using) to the bowl with the vegetable flesh. Season generously with salt and pepper and add a splash more of oil.

4. Fill the vegetable cavities with the stuffing mixture, mounding it slightly. Avoid packing it down (you do not want a hard ball of stuffing). Place the hats back on top of the petits farcis. Arrange them in a baking dish with a little space between vegetables and pour about ½ cup (120 ml) of water in the bottom of the dish. Drizzle the vegetables with olive oil.

5. Bake until the tops are golden brown, the vegetables are tender, and the stuffing is cooked through, about 45 minutes. If the pan juices start to dry up, add a splash of water.

> **NOTE:** *If you wanted to make this dish gluten-free, you could remove the bread crumbs. They make for a nice and light texture, but rice is a good substitute and soaks up the lovely vegetable juices. You can also be very indulgent and use both— my grandma did.*

MOULES-FRITES

SERVES 4 • **PREP TIME:** 10 MINUTES • **COOK TIME:** 20 MINUTES

This restaurant-favorite mussels dish provides dinner and an activity all in one—with everyone gathering around a steaming pot, dunking crusty bread into the aromatic broth, and piling up empty shells as they go. I love adding a splash of pastis for its subtle anise notes, but the classic preparation with just butter and wine is equally luxurious. Either way, the key is plenty of butter to create a rich, golden broth.

4 pounds (1.8 kg) fresh mussels

6 tablespoons salted butter

4 large shallots, finely chopped

6 garlic cloves, finely chopped

1 teaspoon kosher salt

½ teaspoon freshly ground black pepper

3 cups (720 ml) dry white wine

2 tablespoons pastis (optional)

¼ cup (60 ml) heavy cream (optional)

¼ cup (15 g) roughly chopped flat-leaf parsley

French Fries (recipe follows) and crusty bread, for serving

1. Examine the mussels—they should be tightly closed and smell fresh like the sea. If they're open, tap them against the counter and discard any that don't close. Clean under cold water to remove their sand and pull off any stringy beards by tugging them toward the pointed end of the shell.

2. In a large Dutch oven or other heavy pot, melt 4 tablespoons of the butter over medium-low heat. Add the shallots, garlic, salt, and pepper and cook until very soft but not colored, 8 to 10 minutes, stirring occasionally.

3. Increase the heat to high, add the wine and pastis (if using) and bring to a boil for 2 minutes. Add the mussels, give them a good stir, and cover. Steam for about 5 minutes, shaking the pot occasionally and stirring once halfway through, until the mussels have opened up (if any haven't by this point, discard them).

4. Using a slotted spoon, transfer the mussels to a large bowl and cover the bowl to keep them warm. Add the cream to the pot (personally, I like a clear broth, but my whole family fervently disagrees) and simmer for 1 to 2 minutes to bind and reduce the liquid. Whisk in the remaining 2 tablespoons of butter and the parsley, then return the mussels to the pot.

5. Serve immediately in shallow bowls with hot fries and plenty of bread for soaking up all that beautiful broth.

FRENCH FRIES

The only person I have ever known to make French fries from scratch weekly was my grandmother. It was an endeavor for a large table of hungry family members. While prepping the potatoes is time-consuming, the taste is well worth it.

2 pounds (900 g) russet or Yukon Gold potatoes

About ½ inch (1 cm) of neutral oil such as avocado oil, which I like for its clean flavor and high smoke point

Kosher salt

1. Cut the potatoes into thin sticks (about ¼ inch/6 mm thick) and soak them in cold water for at least 20 minutes, then pat dry thoroughly.

2. Heat the oil in a large skillet over medium-high heat (about 375°F/190°C). Working in batches, fry the potatoes until golden and crisp, 6 to 8 minutes, turning once or twice.

3. Transfer to a rack or paper towels to drain and sprinkle generously with salt.

> **NOTE**: If you have an air fryer, just a tiny bit of oil will make this recipe way healthier.

ÉPAULE D'AGNEAU

ROASTED LAMB SHOULDER

SERVES 6 • **PREP TIME:** 20 MINUTES • **COOK TIME:** 4 HOURS

Which region raises the best lamb is a notorious dinner-party argument—the best come from Provence; in my opinion, its meat is extraordinarily tender and sweet. This slow-roasted shoulder is my favorite cut, less formal than a leg but arguably more flavorful. The long, slow cooking with plenty of garlic and honey creates meat so tender you can break it apart with a fork. I prefer to keep the bone in—it helps the meat keep its shape and adds flavor and drama.

¼ cup (60 ml) olive oil

1 bone-in lamb shoulder (3 to 4 pounds / 1.5 kg), trimmed of excess fat

4 garlic cloves, peeled and halved, plus 6 garlic cloves, unpeeled

2 tablespoons salted butter

4 rosemary sprigs

4 thyme sprigs

2 tomatoes, whichever are ripest at the market, cored and halved

1 pound (450 g) small waxy potatoes, peeled and halved

1 pound (450 g) carrots, peeled and cut into large chunks

3 tablespoons honey

½ cup (120 ml) vegetable broth, homemade (see page 6) or store-bought

Kosher salt and freshly ground black pepper

1. Preheat the oven to 300°F.

2. In a large Dutch oven or other heavy pot, heat the olive oil over high heat. Add the lamb and brown thoroughly on all sides, about 10 minutes total. Remove the lamb to a plate and stud it with the halved peeled garlic.

3. Butter the Dutch oven and scatter in the unpeeled garlic cloves, herbs, and tomatoes. Add the lamb and surround it with the potatoes and carrots. Mix the honey with the broth and pour it over everything in the pot. Season generously with salt and pepper.

4. Cover and roast until the meat is falling off the bone, basting occasionally, about 4 hours.

5. To make the jus, remove most of the cooking liquid to a saucepan, reduce over medium heat until syrupy, and pour it back over the meat. The jus will be intense and velvety.

6. Return the pot to the oven, uncovered, for 10 minutes, until the surface is beautifully caramelized and the sauce clings to the meat.

CHOUS FARCIS

STUFFED CABBAGE LIKE LITTLE PILLOWS

SERVES 4 TO 6 • **PREP TIME:** 30 MINUTES • **COOK TIME:** 30 MINUTES

Cabbage is a humble vegetable that transforms into something special when treated right. These stuffed pillows are proof—the leaves become silky as they braise, while the filling stays incredibly juicy. While traditionally made with sausage meat, stuffed cabbage is equally delicious filled with finely chopped mushrooms and a spoonful of white miso. The key is letting the pillows braise slowly in the oven until the cabbage is tender but still holding its bright green color.

1 large Savoy cabbage

¼ teaspoon baking soda (optional, but it will help keep the leaves bright green)

2 garlic cloves, minced

4 tablespoons salted butter, plus more for the baking dish

2 yellow onions, finely diced

¼ cup (60 ml) dry white wine

1 pound (450 g) good-quality pork sausage meat

½ cup (100 g) uncooked white rice or rice of your choice

1 tablespoon tarragon leaves

1 teaspoon smoked paprika

1 teaspoon kosher salt

½ teaspoon freshly ground black pepper

1. Remove 12 large outer leaves from the cabbage, keeping them whole. Finely shred the remaining inner cabbage.

2. Bring a large stockpot of water to a boil over high heat and add the baking soda (if using). Blanch the leaves for 2 to 3 minutes, until pliable. Drain the leaves and pat them dry. Trim the thick part of the stem at the base of each leaf.

3. In a large sauté pan over medium heat, melt 2 tablespoons of the butter. Add the onions, garlic, and shredded cabbage and sauté until soft, 8 to 10 minutes. Add the wine and cook, stirring, until the liquid has reduced by half, about 5 minutes. Add the sausage meat, rice, tarragon, paprika, ½ teaspoon of the salt, and ¼ teaspoon of the pepper.

4. Preheat the oven to 350°F and butter a baking dish that is large enough to hold the pillows comfortably but not too tight.

5. To make a stuffed pillow, lay out one of the cooked cabbage leaves. Place about 3 tablespoons of filling in the center of the leaf. Fold the sides of the leaf over the filling, then fold the bottom of the leaf over and roll it up to enclose completely. Repeat to make the rest of the pillows.

6. Arrange the pillows seam side down in the baking dish. Melt the remaining 2 tablespoons of butter and brush the butter over the pillows. Sprinkle with the remaining ½ teaspoon salt and ¼ teaspoon pepper. Bake for 30 minutes, until the cabbage is tender and slightly bronzed. Serve immediately from the dish.

LE GRAND AIOLI

SERVES 6 • **PREP TIME:** 20 MINUTES • **COOK TIME:** 45 MINUTES

This is the most effortless and luxurious meal all at once—a generous platter of seasonal vegetables and seafood, arranged around a bowl of golden aioli. While traditionally served with salt cod, I love it with gently poached fish and prawns or even just many crudités straight on butcher paper as a large-format grazing table. Everything can be prepared ahead, making this perfect for lazy weekend lunches or standing cocktail parties.

Kosher salt

1 pound (450 g) small waxy potatoes

6 large prawns, shell on

4 carrots, peeled

½ pound (227 g) green beans, trimmed

1 bunch asparagus, trimmed

1 pound (450 g) whitefish fillet, such as cod or haddock, cut into 12 pieces

6 eggs

Aioli Sauce (recipe follows)

1 bunch radishes, trimmed and halved

Dill or fennel fronds, for garnish

1 lemon, cut into wedges, for garnish

1. Line a sheet pan with a clean kitchen towel. Bring a large pot of water to a boil and season aggressively with salt—salty like the sea. Taste it! Lower the heat so that the water is at an energetic simmer. Add the potatoes and cook until tender when pierced with a skewer, 12 to 15 minutes.

2. Remove the potatoes from the water with a slotted spoon and transfer them to the prepared sheet pan to cool. Keep the water at a simmer.

3. Add the prawns to the simmering water and cook until just pink, 3 to 4 minutes. Scoop them out and transfer them to the same sheet pan with the potatoes to cool.

4. In the same simmering water, cook the vegetables, one at a time: the carrots for 8 to 10 minutes, the green beans for 4 to 5 minutes, the asparagus for 3 minutes. You want each to be tender but still have some bite.

5. Gently poach the fish portions in the simmering water until they flake easily, 6 to 8 minutes. Transfer to the sheet pan and let cool to room temperature.

6. Bring the water back to a strong boil. Meanwhile, in a large bowl prepare an ice water bath. Add the eggs to the water and cook for exactly 7 minutes (for jammy centers), then use a slotted spoon to transfer them to the ice water bath to stop the cooking. Peel when cool.

7. Cut the potatoes in half and the carrots in chunks. Set a bowl of the aioli on a large serving platter and surround it with all the components. Garnish with herbs and wedges of lemon.

> **NOTE:** *All the components can be cooked up to 4 hours ahead and kept at room temperature, except for the fish, prawns, and aioli, which should stay chilled until ready to serve.*

AIOLI SAUCE

MAKES ABOUT 1 CUP • **PREP TIME:** 10 MINUTES

Making aioli is easy, but like most sauces whipped by hand, it can be intimidating. It's part of my language of love—when I get home to my family, I make a batch for everyone to enjoy. I'm always hoping it'll last the week to revive the previous night's leftovers and add spark to simply grilled vegetables, but it never, ever lasts more than a meal.

4 garlic cloves

1 teaspoon flaky sea salt, plus more as needed

2 egg yolks

1 tablespoon fresh lemon juice, plus more as needed

1 cup (240 ml) your best olive oil

1. Using a mortar and pestle, crush the garlic with the salt into a smooth paste. If you don't have a mortar, mince the garlic very finely, then use the back of a fork to mash it with the salt until it becomes a paste.

2. Transfer the garlic paste to a medium bowl. Add the egg yolks and lemon juice and whisk until well combined. I love using a mini whisk for this, but a fork works just as well. Add 2 or 3 drops of room-temperature water and whisk—this helps the emulsion get started and makes the aioli light and fluffy.

3. Add the olive oil drop by drop, whisking constantly. When the mixture starts to thicken (after about ¼ cup oil), you can add the oil in a thin, steady stream while continuing to whisk vigorously.

4. When all the oil is incorporated, you will have a thick, golden mayonnaise. Taste and adjust the seasoning with more salt or lemon juice as needed. The aioli will keep in the refrigerator in an airtight container for up to 3 days.

> **NOTE:** *If your aioli breaks, don't panic. Start with a fresh egg yolk in a clean bowl, add a few drops of water, and slowly whisk in the broken aioli. It will come back together.*

RISI E BISI

RISOTTO WITH PEAS

SERVES 4 TO 6 • **PREP TIME:** 15 MINUTES • **COOK TIME:** 25 MINUTES

This is my relaxed approach to risotto: rice and vegetables chopped to approximately the same size soaking up wine and Parmesan on indulgent nights and simple broth on weekdays. Soupy and comforting, this dish is somewhere between a risotto and a rice soup. You can adapt this method to any quick-cooking vegetable: Try asparagus tips in spring, cherry tomatoes in summer, or mushrooms in fall.

½ **stick (60 g) salted butter**

2 **white onions, finely chopped**

8 **cups (2 L) vegetable broth, homemade (see page 6), or store-bought**

2¼ **cups (500 g) carnaroli or arborio rice**

3½ **cups (500 g) fresh or frozen peas**

⅔ **cup (60 g) freshly grated Parmesan, plus more for serving**

Kosher salt and freshly ground black pepper to taste

5 **tablespoons olive oil**

1 **tablespoon finely chopped fresh parsley**

1. In a large saucepan, melt the butter over medium heat. Add the onions and cook until soft and translucent, stirring often, about 5 minutes.

2. Meanwhile, in a medium saucepan, bring the broth to a low simmer.

3. Add the rice to the onions and stir to coat with butter. I know people are obsessed with stirring their risottos constantly, but I'm not

scared of my rice getting a little toasty—color is flavor. Add the warm broth a ladleful at a time, stirring frequently but without getting stressed and waiting for each addition to be absorbed before adding the next.

4. If you're using fresh peas, add them after the rice has cooked about 10 minutes, when it has absorbed about half of the broth and the grains look plump and creamy around the edges but still firm in the center. Continue adding stock and stirring until the rice is tender but still has some bite, 8 to 10 minutes more. If you're using frozen peas, add them when the risotto needs just a few more minutes to cook.

5. Remove the risotto from the heat, stir in the Parmesan, and season well with salt and pepper. Drizzle with the olive oil and gently stir through. The consistency should be looser than a traditional risotto and require a spoon. Garnish with parsley and serve with extra Parmesan.

TIAN PROVENÇALE

SERVES 4 TO 6 • **PREP TIME:** 15 MINUTES • **COOK TIME:** 1½ HOURS

A *tian* is both the name of the earthenware dish and the layered vegetables cooked in it. While this version celebrates summer vegetables, the method adapts to almost anything; my grandmother used to make a rich winter version with potatoes, onions, and Gruyère that I still dream about. Precise measurements aren't crucial here, but try to choose vegetables of similar diameter for the prettiest presentation. A shallow earthenware or ceramic dish works best here—the shallower and longer the better.

2 medium eggplants, ends trimmed

3 medium zucchini, ends trimmed

6 ripe tomatoes, ends trimmed

4 garlic cloves, thinly sliced

⅓ cup (80 ml) olive oil

Leaves from 3 or 4 fresh thyme sprigs

Kosher salt and freshly ground black pepper

1. Preheat the oven to 350°F.

2. Using a mandoline or very sharp knife, slice the eggplants, zucchini, and tomatoes into thin rounds, about ⅛ inch thick. All the vegetables should be roughly the same thickness.

3. Rub a baking dish (see headnote) with a slice of garlic, then scatter all the garlic slices across the bottom. Arrange the vegetable slices vertically on the plate in alternating patterns; they should be tightly packed but not too compressed.

4. Drizzle with the olive oil, sprinkle with thyme leaves, and season well with salt and pepper.

5. Bake, uncovered, for about 1 hour and 15 minutes, until the vegetables are very tender. Add another drizzle of your best olive oil, then serve warm or at room temperature.

RATATOUILLE

SERVES 6 • **PREP TIME:** 15 MINUTES • **COOK TIME:** 1 HOUR

This isn't the fussy, layered version from restaurants—it's the way I learned to make it in Cannes, where each vegetable is cooked separately until properly tender and then married at the end. If you don't have enough pans, cook the water-heavy zucchini with the thirsty eggplant. The result should be silky but still structured, with each vegetable tasting of itself.

2 medium eggplants, trimmed and cut in half lengthwise

2 teaspoons kosher salt, plus more as needed

3 zucchini

2 red bell peppers

1 large yellow onion

Leaves from a few thyme sprigs

4 large ripe tomatoes

¾ cup (180 ml) olive oil, plus more as needed

6 garlic cloves, thinly sliced

Freshly ground black pepper to taste

2 bay leaves

1 small bunch basil

1. Set the eggplant halves in a colander and sprinkle the cut surfaces with salt. Set the colander over the drain in the sink or over a bowl while you cut up the rest of the vegetables: Trim the zucchini and cut it into ½-inch chunks; cut the bell peppers into ½-inch strips, and roughly chop the onion and dice and seed the tomatoes.

2. You'll start cooking with the eggplant first, as it takes the longest. In a large Dutch oven or other heavy pot with a lid, heat ¼ cup of the olive oil over medium-low heat. Rinse and pat the eggplant dry, dice into 1-inch chunks, and add to the pot. Cook until golden and tender, about 25 minutes. Cover the pot if the eggplant starts to dry out.

3. Ideally, you will cook each ingredient separately at the same time. Cook all the vegetables over medium-low heat and stir occasionally to prevent burning, refreshing the olive oil in the pans as needed. (If needed, you can use a single pan and cook the ingredients separately, one after the other.)

4. In a medium saucepan, cook the onion and thyme in ¼ cup of the olive oil until the onion is very soft, about 15 minutes. In a second pan, cook the peppers in the remaining ¼ cup oil until tender, about 12 minutes. In a third pan, cook the zucchini in a thin layer of olive oil until soft, 8 to 10 minutes.

5. Combine all the vegetables in the Dutch oven, add the tomatoes and garlic, and season well with salt and pepper. Simmer gently for 15 minutes.

6. Let cool to room temperature, tear in the basil, and adjust the seasoning as desired. Serve immediately or let cool completely, then refrigerate overnight; like most stewed dishes, this one is even better the day after.

> **NOTE:** *For special occasions, confit each vegetable separately in olive oil in a low oven (275°F) for 3 to 4 hours. Worth every extra minute.*

DESSERTS

Nine-year-old me making crêpes for my little sister, Manon, and all her friends on her seventh birthday.

One of my favorite pages from my grandmother's cookbook—the flan collage looks like a spaceship. I never, ever saw her make a flan!

GÂTEAU AU YAOURT ET FIGUES

YOGURT AND FIG CAKE

SERVES 8 • **PREP TIME:** 20 MINUTES • **COOK TIME:** 35 MINUTES

This is often the first cake French children learn to make, using a yogurt pot as their measuring cup. The recipe has been passed down through generations—mix yogurt, sugar, flour, and oil in the same little pot and somehow it works every time. I prefer to use a 5.3-ounce (125 g) yogurt pot here, but it's easy to scale up if you want to make a larger cake—just use a larger pot to measure all of the ingredients and keep the ratios the same. I've updated my grandmother's recipe with almond flour and a crown of caramelized figs, but the method remains charmingly imprecise.

Unsalted butter, for the pan, plus 2 tablespoons more as needed

4 to 5 ripe fresh figs (any kind will do)

2 tablespoons light or dark brown sugar, as needed

One 5.3-ounce pot (125 g) plain whole milk yogurt

3 large eggs

1 teaspoon pure vanilla extract

One 5.3-ounce yogurt pot (125 ml) olive oil

One 5.3-ounce yogurt pot (125 g) granulated sugar

Two 5.3-ounce yogurt pots (250g) almond flour

Three 5.3-ounce yogurt pots (375g) all-purpose flour

1½ teaspoons baking powder

2 teaspoons kosher salt

1. Preheat the oven to 350°F.

2. Butter a 9-inch round cake pan generously, then line the bottom with parchment paper and butter the paper too. Cut the figs in half and arrange them cut side up on the parchment. The figs will caramelize as they bake, creating a beautiful pattern on top when you flip the cake. If the figs aren't perfectly ripe, sprinkle them

with brown sugar and a dot of butter to help them along.

3. Scrape the yogurt into a large bowl, reserving the empty container. Add the eggs, one at a time, mixing well after each addition. Add the vanilla and olive oil and mix them in.

4. Use the empty yogurt pot to measure the sugar, almond flour, and all-purpose flour and place in a medium bowl. Add the baking powder and salt and whisk to combine.

5. Gradually fold in the dry ingredients into the yogurt mixture until just combined—don't overmix. Pour the batter over the figs.

6. Bake until the cake is golden brown and a knife inserted in the center comes out clean, about 35 minutes.

7. Let cool in the pan for 10 minutes, then run a knife around the edge. Lay a serving plate upside down over the cake, then carefully invert the cake onto the plate. Cut into wedges and serve warm or at room temperature. Keep the cake covered with a kitchen towel at room temperature—it stays tender for about 2 days, though it rarely lasts that long.

Gâteau au Yaourt

BEIGNETS COMME À LA PLAGE

MAKES 8 BEIGNETS • **PREP TIME:** 2 HOURS 30 MINUTES (INCLUDING RISING)
COOK TIME: 20 MINUTES

Along the Riviera, beach vendors weave between umbrellas as they carry trays of these warm beignets, their centers oozing with chocolate or jam. Sticky with sugar and filled with melting chocolate or summer fruits, they're impossible to eat without making a mess—that's half the fun. My favorite version uses a hazelnut spread, but any chocolate spread or fruit filling works.

⅓ cup (70 ml) whole milk, at room temperature

2 teaspoons plus ½ cup (100 g) sugar

2¼ teaspoons active dry yeast

1½ tablespoons unsalted butter

1 large egg, at room temperature

1⅓ cups (160 g) all-purpose flour, plus more for the work surface if needed

¼ teaspoon kosher salt

About 4 cups (1 L) avocado oil or other neutral oil, for the bowl and for frying

½ cup (120 g) hazelnut or chocolate spread, such as Nutella, or jam

Special equipment: piping bag with small tip

1. In a large bowl or in the bowl of a stand mixer fitted with the dough hook, combine the milk, 2 teaspoons of the sugar, and the yeast. Let sit until foamy, about 5 minutes.

2. Melt the butter and let it cool slightly. Add the butter and egg to the yeast mixture and mix well. Add the flour and salt and mix until combined.

3. If not using a stand mixer, lightly flour your work surface. Knead by hand, folding the dough over itself and pushing away with your palm, until the dough is smooth and springs back when gently pressed, about 8 minutes. If using a stand mixer, knead on medium speed until you have the same result.

4. Place the dough in a lightly oiled bowl, cover it with a damp cloth, and let it rise in a warm spot until doubled, about 1½ hours.

5. When the dough has doubled, gently press down on it to release the air bubbles. This step redistributes the yeast and sugar, creating a finer and more delicate texture!

6. Line a sheet pan with parchment paper. Divide the deflated dough into 8 pieces. Roll each into a smooth ball and place it on the prepared sheet pan. Cover with a damp cloth and let rise for another 30 minutes.

7. Line a plate with paper towels. In a large heavy pot, heat 2 inches of oil to 350°F. Fry the beignets in batches until golden brown, about 2 minutes per side. Use tongs to carefully transfer the hot beignets to the prepared plate to drain.

8. Place the remaining ½ cup sugar in a medium bowl. While the beignets are still warm, roll each one in the sugar. Using a small knife, make a little hole in the side of each beignet. Fill a piping bag with hazelnut spread and pipe into each beignet until just filled—you'll feel a slight resistance when they're full.

9. These are best eaten immediately, while the centers are still warm and melty.

CRÊPES À L'ORANGE

MAKES ABOUT 12 CRÊPES • **PREP TIME:** 15 MINUTES • **COOK TIME:** 30 MINUTES

Crêpes were our special dinner when the parents went out—my siblings and I would take turns at the stove, building towering stacks. But my favorite crêpes experience was always at my uncle's restaurant in Cannes, where crêpes Suzette would arrive at the table glistening with citrus and butter. This version swaps the traditional lemon for fresh orange juice and zest and serves them with a cloud of Orange Blossom Whipped Cream (page 184).

FOR THE CRÊPES

Scant 1 cup (120 g) all-purpose flour

3 large eggs

2 teaspoons sugar (for savory crêpes), or 3 tablespoons sugar (for sweet dessert crêpes)

½ teaspoon kosher salt

1¼ cups (300 ml) whole milk

2 tablespoons unsalted butter, melted

2 tablespoons softened unsalted butter or neutral oil, for the pan

FOR THE ORANGE SAUCE

½ stick (60 g) unsalted butter

¼ cup (50 g) sugar

Zest and juice of 2 large oranges (about ½ cup juice)

2 tablespoons Grand Marnier or orange liqueur (optional)

1 batch Orange Blossom Whipped Cream (page 184), for serving

1. PREPARE THE CRÊPES: In a large bowl, whisk together the flour, eggs, sugar, and salt. Gradually pour in the milk, whisking until smooth. Add the melted butter. The batter should be thin, like heavy cream. Cover and refrigerate for 15 minutes or, if you have time, overnight—this rest time helps the flour hydrate, but it's not essential. The batter can be kept in the refrigerator overnight (or for up to 2 days).

2. When the batter has rested, preheat a 10-inch nonstick pan over medium heat. Brush a layer of butter on the heated pan. I use a silicone brush, but you can use a butter-soaked paper towel or clean cloth as well.

3. Pour ¼ cup of the batter into the hot pan, swirling to coat the bottom of the pan with the batter. Swirl and spread the batter along the edge of the pan first, then let the remaining batter settle in the middle of the pan. Make sure the batter is as evenly spread as possible.

Continues

4. Place the pan back on the heat to let the crêpe cook until the edges start to brown and become a little crisp (about 40 seconds). Flip the crêpe over and cook for 10 to 15 seconds on the other side, until the crêpe has caramelized spots. As you finish cooking the crêpes, stack them on a plate. Repeat until all the batter is used up (remember to stir the batter before making each crêpe).

5. PREPARE THE ORANGE SAUCE: In a large skillet over medium heat, melt the butter. Add the sugar and cook, stirring, until it begins to caramelize and turn golden, 3 to 4 minutes. Carefully add the orange zest and juice (it will bubble vigorously). Cook until the sauce thickens slightly, about 2 minutes. Add the Grand Marnier (if using) and cook for another minute.

6. Spoon the warm orange sauce over the crêpes, fold them into quarters and serve immediately with a bowl of the whipped cream on the side.

> **NOTE:** *If the crêpes are no longer warm when you're ready to serve them, place another plate over the stack of crêpes and microwave for about 30 seconds, until the crêpes are warm. Remove the second plate quickly so that the crêpes don't become soggy with steam.*
>
> *The crêpe pan needs to be very hot. For that reason, the first crêpe is almost always a sacrifice to the crêpe gods. Don't be discouraged; just try again.*

SALTED LEMON TART

SERVES 8 • **PREP TIME:** 25 MINUTES • **COOK TIME:** 35 MINUTES

You'll find lemon tarts in every patisserie along the Riviera, but I've come to prefer this version with a saltier crust, which makes the citrus sing. While mine may never look as perfect as the ones at La Merenda, one of my favorite restaurants in Nice, the balance of sweetness, tartness, and saltiness makes it irresistible.

FOR THE CRUST

1½ **cups (180 g) all-purpose flour**

⅓ **cup (65 g) sugar**

1½ **teaspoons kosher salt**

1 **stick (113 g) cold butter, cubed**

1 **large egg**

FOR THE FILLING

4 **lemons**

4 **large eggs**

¾ **cup (150 g) sugar**

1 **stick (113 g) unsalted butter, cubed**

Flaky salt, for finishing

1. PREPARE THE CRUST: In a food processor, pulse the flour, sugar, and salt to combine. Add the cold butter cubes and pulse until the mixture resembles coarse sand. Add the egg and pulse just until the dough comes together.

2. Press the dough evenly into a 9-inch tart pan with a removable bottom and freeze for 30 minutes.

3. Preheat the oven to 375°F. Line the frozen crust with parchment and fill the bottom with pie weights, dried beans, or uncooked rice. Blind bake for 20 minutes, remove the pie weights and parchment, and bake 5 to 10 minutes more, until lightly golden. Let it cool while you make the filling. Lower the oven temperature to 350°F.

4. PREPARE THE FILLING: Zest all four lemons, then juice them—you'll need ½ cup (120ml) juice. In a medium saucepan, whisk together the eggs, sugar, and lemon zest and juice, then add the butter cubes.

5. Cook, whisking constantly, over medium-low heat—this prevents the eggs from scrambling and the butter from separating. Keep whisking until the custard thickens enough to coat the

Continues

back of a spoon and hold a line when you run your finger through it, 5 to 7 minutes. Strain the filling through a fine-mesh sieve into a small bowl. (Don't skip this last step unless you want bits of scrambled egg in your custard!)

6. Pour the warm filling into the cooled tart shell. Bake for 5 minutes, until the filling is just set but still has a slight wobble.

7. Allow the tart to fully cool and set, then sprinkle it with flaky salt. Slice and serve.

MAKE IT YOUR OWN

BLOOD ORANGE FILLING: Use the same amount of fruit juice, but reduce the sugar in the filling to ⅔ cup (135 g), as blood oranges are naturally sweeter than lemons.

GRAPEFRUIT FILLING: The subtle bitterness works beautifully here. Use pink or ruby grapefruit and increase the sugar in the filling to 1 cup (200 g).

My parents had a booth at Les Puces for ten years, and I grew up waking at the crack of dawn most weekends to get to the flea markets early. For this photo shoot, my mom sent my uncle to our location with a truck full of plates and bowls from her armoire. My favorite from her collection is on the cover.

FROZEN RASPBERRY TIRAMISU

SERVES 8 • **PREP TIME:** 25 MINUTES • **FREEZE TIME:** 6 HOURS

My mom is the queen of delicious shortcuts, and this summer dessert might be her best one—a frozen twist on tiramisu that comes together in minutes instead of days. While traditional tiramisu requires patience and precision, this version is pure simplicity: coffee-soaked cookies, jammy raspberries, and clouds of whipped cream, ready to come out of the freezer whenever you want.

2 cups (250 g) fresh or frozen raspberries, plus fresh raspberries, for serving

2 tablespoons sugar

One 7-ounce (200 g) package ladyfingers or amaretti cookies (about 24 cookies)

1 cup (240 ml) strong coffee, cooled

2 cups (500 ml) very cold heavy cream

Cocoa powder, for dusting

1. Place a large bowl and whisk in the freezer for at least 15 minutes to chill.

2. Meanwhile, in a small saucepan, combine the 2 cups raspberries with the sugar and cook over medium-low heat until they break down slightly and become jammy, about 5 minutes. Set them aside to cool completely.

3. Pour the coffee into a medium shallow bowl. Very quickly dunk each ladyfinger in the coffee—they should be just barely moistened so they can also soak up the raspberry juices. Layer half the ladyfingers in a deep 9-inch dish, breaking the pieces to fit if needed. Spread half of the cooled raspberry mixture over the ladyfingers.

4. Remove the bowl and whisk from the freezer and whip the cream until soft peaks form (for more detailed whipping cream instructions, see page 184). Spread half of the whipped cream over the raspberries in an even layer. Repeat the layers: remaining coffee-soaked ladyfingers, remaining raspberry mixture, and remaining whipped cream.

5. Freeze until firm, at least 4 hours or overnight. Remove from the freezer 20 minutes before serving to soften slightly. Dust the top generously with cocoa powder and scatter it with fresh raspberries just before bringing it to the table. Scoop to serve.

> **NOTE:** *Decaf coffee works perfectly here, especially for summer evenings.*
>
> *While this dessert can be made ahead—and it needs to freeze at least 4 hours—the texture is best within the first 48 hours.*

OLIVE OIL CHOCOLATE CAKE

SERVES 8 • **PREP TIME:** 20 MINUTES • **COOK TIME:** 30 MINUTES

This cake sits somewhere between a classic chocolate cake and a fallen soufflé—crackly on top and almost pudding-like inside. The olive oil adds richness and keeps it tender for days, while the mix of melted and chopped chocolate creates pockets of intensity throughout. It's what Sunday afternoons were made for: a little bit of chocolate luxury, just because (and this one happens to be gluten-free!).

½ cup (120 ml) olive oil, plus more for greasing

8 ounces (230 g) 70% dark chocolate, roughly chopped

4 large eggs

1½ cups (180 g) powdered sugar

⅔ cup (60 g) almond flour

Pinch of flaky salt, plus more for serving

1 batch Orange Blossom Whipped Cream (page 184), for serving

1. Preheat the oven to 350°F. Grease an 8-inch cake pan with olive oil on the bottom and sides and line the bottom with parchment paper.

2. Create a double boiler by setting a heatproof bowl over a pan of barely simmering water (the bottom of the bowl shouldn't touch the water). Melt half of the chocolate in the double boiler, keeping the other half for folding in later. (Alternatively, you can melt the chocolate in short bursts in the microwave.)

3. Separate the eggs, putting the egg whites in the bowl of a stand mixer fitted with the whisk attachment and reserving the yolks in a large bowl. Beat the egg whites on medium speed. When they start to foam, gradually add ¾ cup of the powdered sugar. Increase the speed to high

and beat until stiff, glossy peaks form—when you lift the whisk, the peaks should hold their shape, but their tips might gently curl over.

4. Add the remaining ¾ cup powdered sugar to the bowl with the egg yolks and whisk until pale and creamy. Stir in the melted chocolate, olive oil, and salt. Fold in the almond flour and reserved chopped chocolate.

5. Gently fold one-third of the egg whites into the chocolate mixture, then fold in the remaining whites in two additions, using a light hand to keep as much air as possible in the batter. A few white streaks are better than overmixing.

6. Pour the batter into the prepared pan and spread it out evenly and delicately. Bake the cake until it's puffed and crackly on top but still slightly jiggly in the center, about 30 minutes. A toothpick should come out almost clean but the center will remain fudgy.

7. Let the cake cool to room temperature before serving—it will sink as it cools, and this is exactly what you want. Sprinkle with more flaky salt. Cut into slices and serve each with a dollop of the whipped cream. The cake will keep, well-wrapped, at room temperature for several days.

ORANGE BLOSSOM WHIPPED CREAM

MAKES ABOUT 2 CUPS • **PREP TIME:** 5 MINUTES

This ethereal cream is my secret weapon for elevating any dessert—a cloud of orange-scented sweetness that melts over warm chocolate tarts and my Olive Oil Chocolate Cake (page 183) or between layers of Crêpes à l'Orange (page 174). The orange blossom water adds a subtle perfume that reminds me of warm summer evenings in Provence, where the scent of citrus blossoms drifts through open windows. While I keep it barely sweet to complement desserts, feel free to add an extra tablespoon of sugar if serving it on its own with fresh fruit.

1 cup (240 ml) very cold heavy cream
2 tablespoons sugar
1 teaspoon orange blossom water
½ teaspoon pure vanilla extract
Tiny pinch of flaky salt

1. Place the bowl of a stand mixer and the whisk attachment in the freezer for at least 15 minutes—this is nonnegotiable! The colder everything is, the faster the cream will whip and the more stable it will be.

2. Pour the cold cream into the chilled mixer bowl and fit the mixer with the whisk attachment. Add the sugar, orange blossom water, vanilla, and flaky salt. Start the mixer on medium speed. At first the cream will be liquid and splashy. After about 2 minutes, it will start to thicken and leave trails. Watch carefully—the soft peaks should hold their shape but with tips that gently fold over. If you start seeing ripples or waves forming on the surface like a choppy sea, stop immediately—you're just moments away from butter. The cream will hold its shape for several hours in the refrigerator, though it's most luxurious when freshly whipped.

MAKE IT YOUR OWN

- Make plain whipped cream by omitting the orange blossom water.
- Replace the orange blossom water with a splash of rose water.
- Add citrus zest—lemon, orange, or lime.
- Add a splash of amaretto or Grand Marnier for special occasions.
- Use a spoonful of honey instead of sugar.

RUSTIC RHUBARB GALETTE

SERVES 6 TO 8 • **PREP TIME:** 30 MINUTES • **COOK TIME:** 45 MINUTES

A galette is the laid-back European cousin of American pie—all the flavor with none of the fuss. While perfect with practically any peak-season produce, there's no filling I love more than tart rhubarb or, for those few precious weeks in August, apricots at their ambrosial best. The beauty of a galette lies in its imperfection—rough edges are part of its rustic charm, though I'll share my favorite trick: a scattering of sliced almonds around the crust transforms even the most haphazard attempt into something that looks remarkably professional.

1 batch Pâte Brisée (page 16), chilled

All-purpose flour, for the work surface

1 pound (450 g) rhubarb stalks, cut into 2-inch pieces

⅓ cup (65 g) sugar

Zest of 1 orange

1 teaspoon pure vanilla extract

½ cup (45 g) blanched sliced almonds

1 egg, whisked with 1 tablespoon water

2 tablespoons cold unsalted butter, cut into small pieces

Flaky salt

¼ cup (80 g) apricot jam (optional)

1. Preheat the oven to 400°F. Line a sheet pan with parchment paper.

2. Lightly flour your work surface, then roll out the chilled dough into a rough 14-inch round. Don't worry about perfect edges—they're part of the charm. Transfer to the prepared sheet pan.

3. In a large bowl, toss the rhubarb with the sugar, orange zest, and vanilla.

4. Arrange the rhubarb in the center of the dough, leaving a 2-inch border. Fold the edges up and over the filling, pleating as you go. If the edges look a bit rustic, press a few of the sliced almonds all around—they'll toast beautifully as the galette bakes.

Continues

5. Brush the crust with the egg wash and scatter with the remaining almonds. Dot the exposed fruit with butter and sprinkle everything with flaky salt. Bake the galette until the crust is deeply golden and the fruit is bubbling, about 45 minutes.

6. Optional but lovely: While still warm, brush the fruit with jam for a glossy finish.

7. Serve warm or at room temperature. The galette keeps for 1 day at room temperature, covered loosely.

MAKE IT YOUR OWN

- Any fruit in season works here—stone fruits, berries, or even thinly sliced apples.
- For extra crunch, before adding the fruit, sprinkle the crust with ground almonds or hazelnuts.
- A splash of Ghia or white wine in the filling adds lovely complexity.
- If the fruit is very juicy, a spoonful of flour tossed with the sugar helps thicken the juices.

CITRONS GIVRÉS

FROZEN CITRUS

SERVES 4 TO 6 • **PREP TIME:** 30 MINUTES • **FREEZE TIME:** 6 HOURS

While these frozen lemons have become a Riviera cliché on American menus, there's a good reason they've endured—they're a refreshing end to any summer meal and look beautiful nestled on ice. While these are traditionally made with lemons, I often experiment with other citrus—blood oranges need less sugar, whereas grapefruits want a touch more.

6 large lemons, plus 1 for zesting
1 cup (200 g) sugar
2 large egg whites

1. Cut a "hat" off 6 of the lemons at the stem end, about ½ inch from the top, and just enough of the bottom end so the lemons stand upright. Using a small spoon, carefully hollow out the lemons, collecting all the pulp in a bowl. Place the empty lemon shells and their hats in the refrigerator.

2. Press the collected pulp through a fine-mesh sieve to extract as much juice as possible—the back of a spoon can help push it through. Discard the remaining pulp.

3. Finely zest the remaining lemon. In a small saucepan, combine the sugar, zest, and 1 cup (240 ml) water and bring it to a boil over medium heat. Pour it into a medium bowl and set it aside to cool completely. Stir the lemon juice into the cooled syrup.

4. In a medium bowl or the bowl of a stand mixer fitted with the whisk attachment, beat the egg whites until just foamy, then fold them gently into the syrup mixture until combined.

5. If you have an ice cream maker, lucky you! Churn the mixture in the ice cream maker until frozen. If, like me, you don't, pour the mixture into a shallow freezer-safe dish. Freeze for 45 minutes, then remove and vigorously whisk to break up the ice crystals. Repeat this process every 30 to 45 minutes, three to four times total, to create a smooth texture.

6. Fill each chilled lemon shell with the frozen mixture, place the hats on top, and freeze until firm, about 3 hours. Let sit at room temperature for 2 to 3 minutes before serving to make the hats easier to remove. Gently wipe the skin with a clean towel to remove any frost for best presentation. These keep in the freezer for up to 1 week, well wrapped in plastic wrap.

ROASTED PLUM CLAFOUTIS

SERVES 6 TO 8 • **PREP TIME:** 15 MINUTES • **COOK TIME:** 45 MINUTES

Clafoutis is a rustic crustless dessert made by pouring a milky batter over peak summer cherries. Traditionally, cherries are baked with their pits, making it somewhat difficult to eat in front of a crowd, but the pits serve an important purpose: They keep the fruits from loosening too much and making the batter too liquid while it bakes. This recipe can be adapted to pair with any summer fruits, especially blueberries, currants, or raspberries. If I'm using berries or pitted fruit, I prefer to pre-roast them for 15 minutes or so to take some of their moisture away and help the clafoutis keep a nice shape and texture. I prefer a decadent clafoutis, with lots of acidic fruits in a sweet batter.

6 to 8 ripe purple plums, halved and pitted

3 large eggs

1 cup (240 ml) whole milk

½ cup (120 ml) heavy cream

½ cup (100 g) sugar

½ cup (60 g) all-purpose flour

1 teaspoon pure vanilla extract

Butter, for the baking dish

Pinch of kosher salt

Powdered sugar, for serving

1. Preheat the oven to 375°F.

2. Place the plums cut side up in a shallow baking dish and roast until they start to soften and release some of their juices, about 15 minutes.

3. Meanwhile, in a blender or in the bowl of a stand mixer fitted with the whisk attachment, mix together the eggs, milk, cream, sugar, flour, vanilla, and salt on medium speed until completely smooth. Let the batter rest while the plums finish roasting.

4. Butter a 9-inch pie dish or cast-iron skillet. Arrange the warm roasted plums cut side up in the dish. Pour the batter over the fruit—it will float to the top as the clafoutis bakes.

5. Lower the oven temperature to 350°F. Bake until the custard is set but still slightly jiggly in the center, 30 to 35 minutes. The top should be golden brown and puffed around the edges.

6. Let cool slightly; the custard will continue to set as it cools. Dust with powdered sugar and serve warm or at room temperature—this is when the custard is at its most silky.

7. A clafoutis is best served the day it's made, though leftovers can be stored covered in the refrigerator for up to 2 days.

POACHED PEARS AND RICE PUDDING

SERVES 4 TO 6 • **PREP TIME:** 15 MINUTES • **COOK TIME:** 50 MINUTES

This dessert combines two of my childhood favorites, which, I think, are better together: my grandmother's poached fruits (a simple and last-minute dessert) and rice pudding—a humble dish of milk and rice that tastes like comfort. Poaching the pears first ensures they're tender regardless of their ripeness. The key is cooking the rice low and slow to make it thick and velvety. The warm spices and orange zest make the whole thing feel the tiniest bit fancy.

FOR THE PEARS

2½ tablespoons light or dark brown sugar

½ teaspoons ground cinnamon

½ teaspoon pure vanilla extract

6 star anise

3 tablespoons dried hibiscus flowers

6 ripe pears, peeled and halved

FOR THE RICE PUDDING

3 cups milk

1 cup heavy cream

⅓ cup granulated sugar

2 teaspoons finely grated orange zest

1 teaspoon pure vanilla extract

¾ cup uncooked arborio rice

1. PREPARE THE PEARS: In a large saucepan, combine 2 cups water, the brown sugar, cinnamon, vanilla, star anise, and hibiscus flowers. Bring to a simmer over medium heat, stirring until the sugar dissolves. Let simmer for 5 minutes to develop the bright pink color and flavor. Add the pear halves and

gently simmer for 15 to 20 minutes, until tender when pierced with a knife and beautifully pink. Remove the pears with a slotted spoon and set aside to cool. Strain the poaching liquid to remove the hibiscus flowers and star anise, and reserve some of the liquid for serving.

2. PREPARE THE RICE PUDDING: In a medium saucepan combine the milk, cream, granulated sugar, orange zest, and vanilla over medium heat, stirring until the sugar has dissolved. Stir in the rice and bring to a boil, stirring occasionally.

3. Turn the heat to low and simmer until the rice is soft and creamy and the pudding has thickened, stirring occasionally to prevent the rice from sticking to the pan, 30 to 35 minutes. Remove from the heat, cover with a sheet of parchment paper, and let it sit for 10 minutes.

4. To serve, spoon the rice pudding into bowls and serve with the poached pears and a drizzle of the reduced poaching liquid.

PERFECT MERINGUES

MAKES ABOUT 24 SMALL MERINGUES • **PREP TIME:** 15 MINUTES
COOK TIME: 2 HOURS PLUS 1 HOUR COOLING

Meringues might seem intimidating, but they're really just egg whites and sugar, whipped into clouds and dried slowly in the oven. While achieving that pristinely white color in a home oven can be tricky, I'll share all my tips for getting them right. Make them tiny for serving with coffee or larger for the base of a vacherin. Either way, they should be crisp on the outside with just a hint of chewiness in the center. The subtle vanilla note makes them distinctly Riviera.

4 large egg whites, kept at room temperature for at least an hour

Pinch of kosher salt

1 cup (200 g) sugar

½ teaspoon white wine vinegar or fresh lemon juice

¼ teaspoon pure vanilla extract (optional)

1. Preheat the oven to 250°F. Line two sheet pans with parchment paper.

2. Take out a large bowl and check that the bowl is impeccably clean and dry, as any trace of water or fat will prevent your whites from whipping properly. Beat the egg whites and salt on medium speed until foamy like a bubble bath. Gradually add the sugar, about a tablespoon at a time, while beating continuously. When all the sugar is incorporated, increase the speed to medium-high and beat until the meringue is smooth and shiny—when you lift the whisk, the peak should stand straight up like the tip of the Eiffel Tower.

Beat in the vinegar and the vanilla (if using), until just incorporated, 10 to 15 seconds. The acid at this stage helps stabilize the meringue.

3. For small meringues, pipe or spoon 1-inch dollops of egg white onto the prepared sheet pans, leaving space between each. For larger meringues (like those used in pavlova or Vacherin Glacé, page 196), spread the egg whites into an 8-inch round, creating a slight depression in the center.

4. The key to perfectly white meringues is the temperature change: Place the sheet pans in the hot oven and immediately reduce the temperature to 200°F. Leave the oven door slightly cracked open with a wooden spoon—this lets moisture escape and prevents browning. Bake small meringues for 1½ to 2 hours, larger ones for 2 to 2½ hours. They're done when they feel dry and lift easily from the parchment. Perfect meringues should be crisp but not completely dried through—you want that subtle chewiness in the middle.

5. Turn off the oven and let the meringues cool completely inside—this prevents cracking. Meringues will keep for several days in an airtight container at room temperature, but only if it's not humid. On sticky summer days, make them just before serving.

MAKE IT YOUR OWN

- Fold in finely ground almonds or hazelnuts before piping.
- Dust with cocoa powder just before baking.
- Add a drop of rose water instead of vanilla.
- Serve sandwiched with lemon curd, dark chocolate ganache, or Nutella.

TROUBLESHOOTING MERINGUES

- If they brown: Your oven's too hot. Next time, lower the temperature further or prop the door open more.
- If they crack: They cooled too quickly. Let them cool in the oven.

- If they're chewy all the way through: They needed more time in the oven to dry.
- If they weep or become sticky: Humidity got to them! Try again on a drier day.

VACHERIN GLACÉ

SERVES 8 TO 10 • **PREP TIME:** 45 MINUTES • **FREEZE TIME:** 2 HOURS

While pavlova has had its moment, I'll always prefer its frozen cousin, vacherin—the festive French dessert I grew up with. Think shards of crisp meringue layered with ice cream and whipped cream, and sometimes fruits, assembled into a gorgeous mess of textures and topped with sparklers for special occasions. The beauty is in its simplicity: Make the meringues ahead (or even buy them), keep your favorite ice cream on hand, and you can create this showstopper in minutes.

1 quart high-quality ice cream, I like a base of vanilla and another favorite flavor

1 batch Meringues (page 194), made into various sizes

A drizzle of "sauce"—fruit coulis (see Note) pairs well with vanilla and sorbet; melted dark chocolate pairs well with nuttier ice creams

Whipped cream (see Make It Your Own, page 184)

Optional toppings: Fresh berries, edible flowers, and/or sparklers

1. Let the ice cream soften slightly at room temperature. It should be scoopable but not melting. Meanwhile, break the meringues into shards, keeping some whole.

2. Build the vacherin on a serving plate or cake stand, starting with a layer of larger meringues. Add scoops of ice cream, letting them settle into the spaces between meringues. Drizzle with coulis or melted chocolate (if using). Scatter some meringue pieces on top and add dollops of whipped cream. Continue layering,

creating height and texture as you go. The look should be artistic but unfussy, more like the Dolomites than an ice-skating rink.

3. You can either assemble the vacherin right before serving or prepare it up to a day ahead and keep it in the freezer. If making ahead, place the vacherin directly in the freezer after it's assembled and remove from the freezer 5 minutes before serving to soften slightly.

4. Finish with fresh berries, edible flowers, or sparklers for special occasions.

> **NOTE:** *For a quick fruit coulis, blend 2 cups fresh or frozen berries with 2 to 3 tablespoons sugar and a squeeze of fresh lemon juice until smooth. Strain if desired for a silkier texture. Make sure it's completely cool before layering it in. For chocolate sauce, you can either freeze it between layers or drizzle it on right before serving for a dramatic effect.*

MAKE IT YOUR OWN

- Try coffee or chocolate ice cream for a more intense flavor.
- Layer in seasonal fruit compotes (just make sure they cool down before layering them in).
- Swirl in olive oil, salted caramel, or Nutella between layers.
- Add a splash of liqueur to the whipped cream (or use the Orange Blossom Whipped Cream on page 184).

FRUIT CRUMBLE, MANY WAYS

SERVES 6 TO 8 • **PREP TIME:** 20 MINUTES • **COOK TIME:** 45 MINUTES

A crumble is the ultimate adaptable dessert—humble enough for a weeknight, special enough for company. Here I offer two variations: a classic buttery topping and a nutty version that's almost cookie-like in texture. The latter began as an attempt to make it gluten-free for friends but became a favorite in its own right (see Make It Your Own for a fully gluten-free topping). Each celebrates whatever fruits need using—in summer, berries and stone fruits; in fall, apples and pears; in winter, frozen fruits from warmer days; and in spring, my absolute favorite, rhubarb and berries. The key is getting the right balance of sweet and tart fruits and letting them bubble until they're jammy beneath their crisp lid.

FOR THE FILLING

1½ pounds (700 g) mixed fruit (stone fruits should be pitted and sliced into 1-inch pieces; apples should be peeled, cored, and cut into 1-inch pieces; berries can be left whole)

⅓ cup (65 g) sugar

Zest and juice of 1 lemon

1 teaspoon kosher salt

FOR THE CLASSIC TOPPING

1 cup (120 g) all-purpose flour

⅔ cup (120 g) sugar

1 teaspoon kosher salt

1 stick (113 g) plus 1 tablespoon cold unsalted butter, cubed

FOR THE HAZELNUT TOPPING

½ cup (60 g) all-purpose flour

⅔ cup (60 g) hazelnut flour (optional) or all-purpose flour

⅔ cup (120 g) sugar

1 teaspoon kosher salt

1 stick (113 g) plus 1 tablespoon cold unsalted butter, cubed

½ cup (70 g) hazelnuts, roughly chopped

1. Preheat the oven to 375°F.

2. PREPARE THE FILLING: In a 9-inch baking dish, pie plate, or cast-iron skillet, toss the fruits with the sugar, lemon zest and juice, and salt.

3. PREPARE EITHER TOPPING: In a medium bowl, mix the flour (and hazelnut flour, if using, for the hazelnut topping), sugar, and salt. Work in the cold butter cubes with your fingertips until the mixture feels like coarse sand with some bigger buttery crumbs (this texture is what creates those lovely craggy bits on top). Add the roughly chopped hazelnuts.

4. Scatter the topping evenly over the fruit and tuck in some extra in the corners—it will get deliciously crispy. Bake the crumble until the fruit is bubbling at the edges and the topping turns golden brown, about 45 minutes. Let cool slightly to give the filling time to set before serving.

MAKE IT YOUR OWN

- Mix and match fruits based on what's in season—try combining tart and sweet varieties.
- If the fruit you're using is very juicy, mix in 2 tablespoons cornstarch with the sugar to help thicken the juices as it bakes.
- Add warming spices like cinnamon, nutmeg, or cardamom to the filling, or a splash of vanilla.
- For a fully gluten-free version, replace the all-purpose flour with a mix of nut flour and rice flour. While the crumble won't be quite as crispy as with all-purpose flour, the rice flour helps achieve a nice crunch.

CHOCOLATE CLOUD MOUSSE

SERVES 6 • **PREP TIME:** 25 MINUTES • **CHILL TIME:** 3 HOURS

Chocolate mousse is my father's favorite dessert, so I spent years perfecting this recipe. Two things make it impossibly light: the ratio of yolks to whites (for every four yolks, I use five whites) and careful tempering—letting the chocolate cool until it's just warm before folding in the whites, so they stay cloudlike instead of deflating. I love serving this mousse in a large bowl that gets passed around the dinner table with a silver spoon—there's something special about sharing dessert this way. Just make sure to use the best-quality dark chocolate you can find; it really makes all the difference.

7 ounces (200 g) dark chocolate (at least 50% cacao), roughly chopped

3½ ounces (100 ml) heavy cream

2 ounces (60 g) sugar

4 large eggs plus 1 egg white, room temperature

Tiny pinch of kosher salt

Flaky salt (optional), for serving

1. Create a double boiler by setting a heatproof bowl over a pan of barely simmering water (the bottom of the bowl shouldn't touch the water). Melt the chocolate with the cream and sugar, stirring occasionally until smooth. Remove from the heat and let cool until just warm to the touch.

2. Separate the eggs, making sure no yolk gets into the whites—even a tiny bit of yolk will keep them from whipping properly. Add the yolks one by one to the cooled chocolate mixture, mixing well between each addition.

3. In a clean, dry bowl using a hand mixer or in the bowl of a stand mixer fitted with the whisk attachment, whisk the egg whites with the kosher salt until foamy. Continue beating until stiff— when you lift the whisk, the peaks should stand straight up.

4. Lighten the chocolate base by adding a spoonful of egg whites. Gently fold in the rest of the egg whites in two additions until just combined. You'll know it's ready when you can't see any more white streaks, but better to keep a few white streaks than risk overmixing.

5. Pour the mousse into a serving bowl or divide it between individual dishes. Refrigerate for at least 3 hours or overnight. Sprinkle with flaky salt (if using) and serve.

NOTE: *The mousse will keep, covered with plastic wrap, for up to 2 days in the refrigerator, though it's most ethereal the day it's made.*

ÎLE FLOTTANTE

FLOATING ISLAND

SERVES 4 TO 6 • **PREP TIME:** 30 MINUTES • **COOK TIME:** 20 MINUTES

Pillowy clouds of meringue floating on a sea of vanilla custard—our French version of eggnog. Unlike the crisp, dried meringues used in Vacherin, these are gently poached until just set, creating soft, cloudlike pillows. While it might look fancy, it's an easy dessert to make for a crowd. It's naturally gluten-free and adaptable—I love garnishing mine with both caramelized almonds and delicate shards of spun sugar for a double dose of crunch, but French praline, coconut, or chocolate chips make fun additions too.

FOR THE VANILLA CUSTARD (CRÈME ANGLAISE)

1 vanilla bean

2 cups (480 ml) whole milk

4 large egg yolks

½ cup (100 g) sugar

Pinch of kosher salt

FOR THE MERINGUE ISLANDS

4 large egg whites, at room temperature

Pinch of kosher salt

½ cup (100 g) sugar

FOR THE CARAMEL DECORATIONS

½ cup (100 g) sugar

FOR THE CARAMELIZED ALMONDS

¼ cup (50 g) sugar

½ cup (70 g) whole almonds

1. PREPARE THE CUSTARD: Split the vanilla bean lengthwise and scrape out the seeds. In a medium saucepan, bring the milk, salt, and vanilla bean pod with its scraped seeds to a simmer over medium heat—do not boil. Remove from the heat and let steep for 10 minutes.

2. Meanwhile, in a medium bowl whisk the egg yolks and sugar until pale and creamy. Through a strainer, slowly add the warm milk to the egg-sugar mixture, whisking constantly. Discard the vanilla bean pod. Return the mixture to the pan and cook over low heat, stirring constantly in a figure-eight motion with a wooden spoon. The custard is ready when it coats the back of the spoon and holds a line when you run your finger through it, and it has no more foam on the surface, 8 to 10 minutes. Strain into a bowl and cover with plastic wrap pressed directly onto the surface. Chill for at least 2 hours.

3. PREPARE THE MERINGUE ISLANDS: Preheat the oven to 250°F. Line a sheet pan with parchment paper.

4. In the very clean, very dry bowl of a stand mixer fitted with the whisk attachment, beat the egg whites with a pinch of salt on medium-low until frothy, about 2 minutes. Tighten them by adding ¼ cup of the sugar and gradually increasing the speed to medium-high. Increase the speed to high while slowly pouring in the remaining ¼ cup sugar and beat until the egg whites are stiff and glossy, 3 to 4 minutes.

5. Spoon or pipe large dollops of meringue (about ½ cup each) onto the prepared sheet pan. Bake for 15 to 20 minutes, until set on the outside but still marshmallowy inside. They should be barely colored. Transfer to a wire rack to briefly cool.

6. PREPARE THE CARAMEL DECORATIONS:
Lay a sheet of parchment paper on your work surface. In a small light-colored saucepan, heat the sugar over medium heat without stirring. When it is melted and amber-colored, drizzle it in thin ribbons onto parchment paper, making decorative shapes or jumbled filaments. This may be tricky the first time, but you'll get the hang of it. Let cool until set completely.

7. PREPARE THE ALMONDS: Lay a fresh sheet of parchment paper on your work

surface. In the same saucepan that was used to make the caramel, heat the sugar over medium heat until melted. Add the almonds and stir to coat them completely. Spread out the almonds on parchment to cool.

8. To serve, pour the chilled custard into dessert glasses or bowls. Add a floating meringue island, then top with caramelized almonds and a shard of caramel decoration.

> **NOTE:** *The custard can be made a day ahead. Caramel decorations and almonds can be made a few hours in advance if kept in a dry place. Meringues are best served shortly after baking.*

CAFE
GOURMAND

I don't ever remember having a bedtime, and
my parents took me everywhere they went. If my
grandmother was around, I would be allowed on
her lap and given biscotti to teethe on until
my eyes closed by themselves.

All the little biscuits and cookies would be
kept in tin boxes and opened up in the evening
or after lunch to be dipped in tea while
cozying up with a book or the TV. Dolce far
niente, but with dolci!

BACI DI DAMA

MAKES ABOUT 24 SANDWICH COOKIES • **PREP TIME:** 45 MINUTES • **COOK TIME:** 25 MINUTES

Of all the treats that appear on espresso saucers, these tiny "lady's kisses" from northern Italy might be my favorite. The ground hazelnuts create a delicate, almost sandy crumb that melts the moment it hits your tongue. While they are traditionally filled with ganache, I often reach for Nutella to bind them. A couple alongside your espresso is all you need, which makes them perfect for café gourmand. Though I'll admit I've been known to sneak them straight from the tin.

1 cup (140 g) hazelnuts

¾ cup (85 g) powdered sugar

1 cup (120 g) all-purpose flour

¼ teaspoon kosher salt

1 stick (113 g) cold unsalted butter, cut into 1/2-inch cubes

1 teaspoon pure vanilla extract or dark rum

1 teaspoon finely grated lemon zest (from about half a lemon)

4 ounces (113 g) semi-sweet or bittersweet chocolate (60% to 70% cacao), roughly chopped, or Nutella (see Note)

1. Arrange racks in the bottom and upper third of the oven and preheat the oven to 350°F. Line two sheet pans with parchment paper.

2. Spread the hazelnuts on one of the prepared pans and toast until deeply fragrant, about 10 minutes. While they are still warm but cool enough to handle, wrap them in a clean damp tea towel and rub vigorously to remove as many skins as possible. Don't worry if some stubborn bits remain.

3. Transfer the warm hazelnuts to a food processor with 2 tablespoons of the powdered sugar. Process until finely ground, 1 to 2 minutes. Add the remaining powdered sugar, the flour, and salt, pulsing until well combined.

Add the butter cubes, vanilla, and lemon zest and process until the dough comes together, about 30 seconds.

4. Turn out the dough onto a work surface and divide it into 4 equal pieces. Roll each into a 12 × 1-inch log. Cut each log into 24 half-inch pieces and roll the pieces into balls. Space them an inch apart on the prepared sheet pans. It's okay if they are a little snug.

5. Bake for 8 minutes, then rotate the pans between the racks and front to back. Continue baking until the tops are dry and edges just start to turn golden, about 6 minutes more. Set aside to cool completely on the pans.

6. Place the chocolate in a microwave-safe bowl and melt it in 30-second microwave bursts, stirring between each, until smooth. Dollop about ½ teaspoon onto the flat side of a cookie and sandwich with another, matching sizes as best you can. Let set at least 15 minutes before serving.

> **NOTE:** *Store the cookies in an airtight container for up to 1 week, though they rarely last that long in my house. If you're using Nutella instead of chocolate, slightly warm it for easier spreading.*

ALMOND BISCOTTI

MAKES ABOUT 36 COOKIES • **PREP TIME:** 20 MINUTES • **COOK TIME:** 45 MINUTES

Biscotti means "twice-cooked" in Italian, and that second bake is what gives these cookies their characteristic crunch. They're meant to be dunked—in coffee, in wine, or, if you're feeling particularly Italian, in vin santo. I love making a big batch on Sunday afternoons; the rhythmic slicing and the anise-scented kitchen signal the start of a slower-paced evening. They're also the sturdiest cookies in my repertoire, perfect for care packages or keeping in a tin for unexpected visitors.

2 cups (255 g) all-purpose flour

1 cup (200 g) sugar

½ teaspoon kosher salt

2 teaspoons baking powder

1 teaspoon anise extract (optional)

2 eggs plus 1 egg yolk

1 cup (155 g) whole almonds, skin on

1. Preheat the oven to 350°F. Line a sheet pan with parchment paper and set aside.

2. In a large bowl, mix together the flour, sugar, salt, and baking powder. Make a well in the center and add the eggs, egg yolk, and anise. Knead until the dough comes together, about 1 minute. Add the almonds and mix just until distributed.

3. Transfer the dough to the prepared sheet pan. The dough will be sticky; resist the urge to add more flour! Shape the dough into three 12 × 1¼-inch logs and flatten into ovals about ¾ inch high. Space them 2 inches apart on the pan. Bake until golden brown, about 30 minutes. The logs will still be soft—let them cool for 10 minutes.

4. Lower the oven temperature to 300°F.

5. Using a sharp knife, cut each log diagonally into 12 slices. Lay the slices cut side down on the sheet pan—at this point, minimum spacing is needed and they should all fit. Bake for about 15 minutes, until they're crisp and lightly golden.

6. Let the biscotti cool completely—they'll continue to crisp as they cool. These keep for weeks in an airtight container at room temperature, though they rarely last that long in my house.

MAKE IT YOUR OWN

- Swap the almonds for pistachios or hazelnuts.
- Add dark chocolate chips or orange or lemon zest to the dough.
- Replace the anise extract with amaretto for more intense almond flavor.
- After the second bake, dip one end of each cookie in melted chocolate.

ORANGETTES

CANDIED ORANGE PEEL DIPPED IN CHOCOLATE

MAKES ABOUT 40 PIECES • **PREP TIME:** 30 MINUTES • **COOK TIME:** 1 HOUR PLUS OVERNIGHT DRYING

In France, these chocolate-dipped candied peels seemed to materialize everywhere—tucked alongside espresso cups, wrapped in cellophane as gifts, or piled in crystal bowls at my grandmother's house. While orange is the classic choice (and arguably perfect), I can't resist making them with thin strips of lemon, grapefruit, or my mother's favorite: ginger.

3 large organic oranges

2 cups (400 g) sugar, plus more for coating

1 vanilla bean, split (optional)

8 ounces (225 g) dark chocolate (70% cacao), roughly chopped

1. Gently wash the oranges with a vegetable brush. Using a sharp knife, score the peel into quarters from top to bottom. Carefully remove the peel one quarter at a time, then slice each into strips about ¼ inch wide.

2. Blanch the peels to remove any bitterness and ensure that the final candied peels are tender: Place the strips in a medium saucepan and cover with cold water. Bring to a boil, then drain immediately. Repeat this process twice more, then remove the peels to a plate.

3. In the same saucepan, combine the sugar and 2 cups (480 ml) water. Add the vanilla bean (if using) and bring to a simmer over low heat, stirring until the sugar dissolves. Add the blanched peels and let them simmer very gently until they become translucent and the syrup thickens, about 45 minutes. You want a very gentle bubble—too vigorous and the peels

will toughen. They're done when a piece bends easily without breaking.

4. Set a wire rack over a sheet of parchment paper on your work surface. Using a slotted spoon, transfer the peels to the wire rack. Save that aromatic syrup, it's wonderful in cocktails! Let the peels dry overnight or for at least 8 hours.

5. When the peels are fully dry, roll them in additional sugar if you like, though I often skip this step when I'm planning to dip them in chocolate. Either way, they're delicious.

6. Create a double boiler by setting a heatproof bowl over a pan of barely simmering water (the bottom of the bowl shouldn't touch the water). Melt two-thirds of the chocolate, remove from the heat, and stir in the remaining chocolate until smooth and slightly cooled. Dip each candied peel halfway into the chocolate, letting excess drip off. Place it on parchment to set.

7. Store the orangettes in a tin, layered between sheets of parchment to protect the chocolate coating. They will keep for about 1 week.

CHOCOLATE-DIPPED HEARTS

MAKES 24 SMALL HEARTS • **PREP TIME:** 20 MINUTES PLUS 30 MINUTES CHILLING
COOK TIME: 12 TO 15 MINUTES

While most café gourmand treats are elaborate little works of art, these hearts prove that sometimes less is more—just butter, flour, and sugar transformed into crisp, delicate cookies that shatter at first bite. The chocolate dip isn't strictly traditional, but it makes them feel special enough for company while still being enough for everyday indulgence.

2 cups (240 g) all-purpose flour, plus more for the work surface

½ cup (60 g) powdered sugar

¼ teaspoon flaky salt, plus more for sprinkling

2 sticks (225 g) cold unsalted butter, cubed (see Note)

1 teaspoon pure vanilla extract

6 ounces (170 g) dark chocolate (70% cacao)

Special equipment: 1½-inch heart-shaped cookie cutter or other small cutter

1. In a food processor, pulse the flour, powdered sugar, and flaky salt to combine. Add the butter cubes and vanilla, then pulse until the mixture just starts to come together. It should hold when pressed but still look somewhat crumbly. Don't overwork it or your cookies will be tough.

2. Lightly flour your work surface, then turn out the dough and gently knead it into a disk. Wrap tightly in plastic wrap and chill for at least 30 minutes, until firm enough to roll.

3. Preheat the oven to 350°F. Line two sheet pans with parchment paper.

4. On a floured work surface, roll out the chilled dough to about ¼ inch thick. Cut out cookies using a small heart-shaped cutter (my cutter is 1½ inches across). Reroll the scraps to continue cutting just once—after that the dough

tends to get tough. Place the hearts about 1 inch apart on the prepared sheet pans.

5. Bake for 12 to 15 minutes, until the edges of the cookies are just beginning to turn golden. Let cool completely on the sheet pans.

6. Create a double boiler by setting a heatproof bowl over a pan of barely simmering water (the bottom of the bowl shouldn't touch the water). Melt the chocolate, stirring occasionally, until melted and smooth. (Alternatively, you can melt the chocolate in short bursts in a small microwave-safe bowl in the microwave, stirring between each.)

7. Lay a sheet of parchment paper on your work surface. Dip one side of each heart into the chocolate, letting the excess drip off. Place the hearts on the parchment paper and sprinkle with flaky salt (if using). Let the chocolate set completely before serving or storing.

8. These keep beautifully in an airtight container at room temperature for about 1 week. Layer them between sheets of parchment to protect the chocolate coating.

> **NOTE:** *The success of these cookies depends entirely on your butter—use the best you can find. European-style butter, with its higher fat content, will give you the crumbliest, most delicate texture.*

MAKE IT YOUR OWN

- Add orange or lemon zest to the dough.
- Replace the vanilla extract with almond extract.
- Use milk chocolate for dipping.
- Sprinkle the chocolate with chopped pistachios before it sets.
- Add dried culinary lavender buds to the sugar before mixing.
- Drizzle with white chocolate.

PÂTES DE FRUITS

MAKES ABOUT 64 PIECES • **PREP TIME:** 30 MINUTES • **COOK TIME:** 25 MINUTES PLUS OVERNIGHT SETTING

In France, these jewel-toned fruit jellies are a patisserie staple lined up in pristine rows behind glass. While they might look intimidating, they're really just fruit, sugar, and pectin, cooked down until concentrated and set until firm. I love making them with whatever fruit looks best at the market, though nothing beats classic raspberry or apricot.

2 cups (500 g) fresh or frozen fruit (see Note)

2 cups (500 g) sugar, plus more for coating

For low-pectin fruits, 1 ounce (25 g) pectin: berries, peach, cherry, mango, passion fruit, fig, melon

For high-pectin fruits, ½ ounce (15 g) pectin: apple, quince, plum, apricot, citrus, gooseberry, green grape

2 tablespoons fresh lemon juice

Pinch of kosher salt

Hot water, for the knife

1. Line an 8-inch square pan with parchment paper, leaving an overhang for easy removal.

2. Puree the fruit. If using berries: Puree until smooth, then strain to remove seeds. You should have about 2 cups of puree. If using firm fruits: Peel, core, and seed the fruit, as appropriate, and cut it into slices or chunks. Place the fruit in a medium saucepan, add a splash of water, cover the pan, and cook over medium heat until very soft (the timing will depend on the fruit—check and stir often). In a blender or food processor, puree the fruit, then strain it through a fine-mesh sieve into a small bowl, pressing it through with the back of a spoon to get every drop. Do not skip the straining process.

3. In a large heavy-bottomed pot, whisk together the sugar and appropriate amount of pectin until combined. Add the fruit puree, lemon juice, and salt and cook over medium heat, stirring constantly with a heatproof spatula, until the mixture reaches 223°F on a candy thermometer. The mixture should be glossy and pull away from the sides of the pan slightly.

4. Pour the mixture immediately into the prepared pan, smoothing the top. Let set at room temperature overnight.

5. The next day, lift the pâtes de fruits from the pan using the parchment overhang. Cut it into 1-inch squares using a sharp knife dipped in hot water between cuts. Roll each piece in sugar. Store in an airtight container at room temperature for up to 2 weeks.

> **NOTE:** *Frozen fruit works beautifully. Just let it thaw completely before using. It might need a few extra minutes of cooking to concentrate the flavors. Avoid very soft or watery fruits (such as watermelon or banana), which won't set well.*

MAKE IT YOUR OWN

APRICOT-LAVENDER: Add 1 teaspoon dried culinary lavender to the sugar.

PEAR-VANILLA: Add the seeds from 1 vanilla bean to the sugar.

BLOOD ORANGE–CAMPARI: Replace the lemon juice with Campari.

RASPBERRY-LYCHEE: Use half raspberry, half lychee puree.

DRINKS

From one of my favorite Ghia campaigns.
Shot by Alex Paganelli.

SHRUBS, MANY WAYS

MAKES ABOUT 1 QUART • **PREP TIME:** 20 MINUTES • **COOK TIME:** 10 MINUTES

Before I created Ghia, I was constantly looking for ways to have interesting nonalcoholic pairings to kick-start my evenings. Shrubs are an easy way to use the best of the market without compromising on complexity: They're effectively infused drinking vinegars mixed with bubbles—you can add a splash of alcohol, too—so they're tart, sweet, and acidic all at once.

A ratio of 1:1:1 for fruit, sweet, and vinegar is where most shrub recipes start, but I tend to prefer mine less sweet, especially when fruits are at their peak. The cooking step is optional when using fruits with softer flesh, but roasting or cooking them is a great way to naturally get the fruit sugar to develop, and subsequently cut down on sugar content.

2 cups (300 g) fresh berries, such as strawberries, raspberries, or blackberries, hulled and sliced if necessary

1 cup (200 g) sugar

6 basil sprigs

2 cups (475 ml) apple cider vinegar

Sparkling water, to top

1. Combine the berries, sugar, and basil in a medium bowl and muddle until liquid starts to emerge. If using firmer berries like blueberries, cook them with the sugar in a covered saucepan with a splash of water over medium heat until very soft, about 5 minutes, then let cool completely. Transfer to a medium bowl.

2. Add the apple cider vinegar, cover the bowl, and refrigerate for at least 1 week.

3. Strain the mixture into a separate medium bowl through a fine-mesh sieve, extracting as much of the juice as you can. The pulp can be discarded or reused (it's a great topping for oatmeal).

4. When ready to serve, mix 2 ounces (¼ cup) of the shrub with 8 ounces (1 cup) of sparkling water. Store the shrub concentrate in a airtight container in the refrigerator for up to 1 month.

OTHER GREAT SHRUB COMBINATIONS

Pineapple, raw sugar, cloves, white vinegar

Orange, honey, thyme, white or apple cider vinegar

Lemon, white sugar, mint, apple cider vinegar

TANGERINE-THYME SHRUB

MAKES ABOUT 2 CUPS • **PREP TIME:** 10 MINUTES • **COOK TIME:** 5 MINUTES
RESTING TIME: 1 TO 2 DAYS (SEE NOTE)

During the winter, when tangerines tumble across market stalls like tiny suns, I make this shrub by the gallon. There's something almost alchemical about a shrub—the way time makes the flavors intertwine. Let it rest for a day or two and the taste will become more than the sum of its parts.

½ cup (70 g) honey

3 fresh thyme sprigs, plus more for garnish

1 cup (240 ml) freshly squeezed tangerine juice, strained (from about 6 tangerines)

¼ to ½ cup (60 ml to 120 ml) apple cider vinegar

Sparkling water

Ice cubes

Tangerine slice, for garnish

1. In a small saucepan over medium heat, combine the honey, thyme, and 1 cup (240 ml) water. Stir occasionally until the honey dissolves and the liquid reduces slightly, about 5 minutes. Remove from the heat and let the thyme steep for 5 minutes, then discard the thyme.

2. Add the tangerine juice and ¼ cup (60 ml) vinegar. Taste and add more vinegar if desired; remember that the flavors will mellow as the shrub rests. Transfer to a clean bottle, seal, and refrigerate.

3. To serve, fill a festive glass with ice cubes. Mix 1 part shrub with 2 to 3 parts sparkling water and pour over the ice. Garnish with fresh thyme and a slice of tangerine.

4. This shrub will keep for up to 1 month in the refrigerator, though the bright citrus notes are best in the first 2 weeks.

> **NOTE:** *The beauty of shrubs lies in patience. Give it at least a day or two in the refrigerator for the vinegar to mellow and the flavors to harmonize completely.*

Salt and Smoke
Grapefruit
Spritz

Tangerine-Thyme
Shrub

Classic Ghia
Spritz

SALT AND SMOKE GRAPEFRUIT SPRITZ

SERVES 1 • **PREP TIME:** 5 MINUTES

There's a particular pleasure in the ritual of this drink—the fragrant fog of rosemary smoke, the gentle pop as grapefruit caramelizes under flame. It transforms my kitchen into a late-night bar along the Riviera, if only for a moment.

1 rosemary sprig

Ice

1½ ounces (45 ml) Ghia Original Aperitif

2 ounces (60 ml) ruby red grapefruit juice, strained

½ ounce (15 ml) fresh lime juice, strained

¼ ounce (7 ml) simple syrup, plus more for brushing (see Note)

Pinch of flaky salt

1½ ounces (45 ml) soda water

1 grapefruit slice

1. Using a culinary torch, light the tip of your rosemary sprig until it starts to smoke. Place it on a wooden board and quickly invert a coupe or rocks glass over it to capture the smoke. Reserve the rosemary sprig for the garnish.

2. Meanwhile, in a cocktail shaker filled halfway with ice,combine the Ghia, both citrus juices, the simple syrup, and the flaky salt. Shake vigorously until well chilled, about 15 seconds.

3. Turn the smoked glass upright and fill it with fresh ice. Double strain the mixture over the ice and top with soda water.

4. For the garnish, brush a grapefruit slice lightly with simple syrup and torch it briefly until caramelized in spots. Add to the glass along with the smoked rosemary sprig.

> **NOTE:** *To make simple syrup, combine equal parts sugar and water in a small saucepan. Bring to a simmer, stirring until sugar dissolves. Let cool completely before using. Store in an airtight container in the refrigerator for up to 1 month.*
>
> *For a less sweet version, skip the simple syrup in the drink and rely on the natural sweetness of the grapefruit juice. The caramelized garnish will still provide a lovely contrast.*

GHIA + RHUBARB SUNSET PUNCH

MAKES ABOUT 1 GALLON • **PREP TIME:** 30 MINUTES • **COOK TIME:** 15 MINUTES PLUS OVERNIGHT CHILLING

Here's a bright, celebratory punch that isn't too sweet and showcases the tart complexity of rhubarb against our original Ghia aperitif's botanical backbone. The addition of citrus and seasonal garnishes makes this a showstopping centerpiece. The ruby color of the rhubarb syrup creates a stunning ombré effect as it settles into the punch bowl, making each ladle a slightly different shade of sunset. This punch works just as well year-round using frozen rhubarb, and the rhubarb syrup can be made a week ahead, making this punch as effortless as it is delightful.

FOR THE PUNCH

Three 500 ml bottles Ghia Original Aperitif

6 cups (1.4 L) club soda

Ice spheres or cubes

1 batch (890 ml) Rhubarb Syrup (see below)

2½ cups (590 ml) fresh lemon juice, strained

FOR THE RHUBARB SYRUP

4 cups (400 g) roughly chopped rhubarb, fresh or frozen

2 cups (400 g) sugar

FOR THE GARNISH

Orange and lemon wheels

Pink peppercorns

Fresh citrus leaves

1. The night before your gathering, set the stage by chilling the Ghia and club soda in the refrigerator.

2. The next day, make the rhubarb syrup. In a large saucepan, let the rhubarb, sugar, and 2 cups (475 ml) water melt into each other over medium heat, stirring occasionally as the mixture transforms. You'll know it's ready when the rhubarb has completely surrendered its structure, about 15 minutes. Strain the ruby elixir through a fine-mesh sieve into a medium bowl. Set it aside to cool, then transfer to a clean bottle, seal, and refrigerate. It will keep in the refrigerator for 1 week.

3. When ready to serve, build the punch. Set a punch bowl on a centrally located table (you won't want to move it). Begin by adding the ice spheres, then layer in the Ghia, the rhubarb syrup, and lemon juice. Finally, add the club soda. Garnish with citrus wheels, peppercorns, and citrus leaves—this is as much about beauty as it is about flavor.

WHITE BALSAMIC STRAWBERRY SPRITZ

SERVES 4 TO 6 (4- TO 6-OUNCE SERVINGS) • **PREP TIME:** 10 MINUTES
REST TIME: AT LEAST 30 MINUTES

Sweet meets tart in this summer Spritz, where white balsamic vinegar coaxes out strawberries' deeper notes. The syrup balances bright fruit and subtle acidity, and the macerated berries make a great snack while mixing drinks.

FOR THE MACERATED STRAWBERRIES

1 cup (225 g) strawberries, hulled and roughly chopped

½ cup (100 g) sugar

2 tablespoons white balsamic vinegar

FOR EACH DRINK

Ice cubes

2 ounces (60 ml) fresh lemon juice

1 ounce (30 ml) macerated strawberry syrup

4 to 6 ounces (120 ml to 180 ml) sparkling water

1 spoonful macerated strawberries

1. PREPARE THE STRAWBERRIES: Combine the chopped strawberries, sugar, and white balsamic vinegar in a small bowl. Stir gently to coat, then let sit at room temperature for at least 30 minutes or up to several hours. If making ahead, refrigerate after the first hour. The longer they rest, the more intense the flavors become. Strain the berries from their syrup, keeping both.

2. FOR EACH INDIVIDUAL SERVING: Fill a glass with ice cubes. Add the lemon juice and syrup, then top with sparkling water. Add a spoonful of the macerated strawberries on top and serve with a straw.

3. FOR A PITCHER SERVING SIX: Combine 6 ounces (180 ml) strawberry syrup with 12 ounces (360 ml) lemon juice in a pitcher. Just before serving, add ice cubes and 24 to 30 ounces (710 to 900 ml) sparkling water. Stir gently and serve with spoonfuls of macerated strawberries added to each glass as you serve.

> **NOTE:** *You can substitute any other berries for the strawberries in this recipe. And while you probably won't need any ideas for how to use up leftover macerated berries, just know they're particularly good on ice cream or over cake.*

CLASSIC GHIA SPRITZ

SERVES 1 • **PREP TIME:** 2 MINUTES

Back when I used to drink alcohol, I loved the simplicity and bitterness of a Campari soda at sunset—and this drink takes me back to that. This is the easiest way to enjoy Ghia—a bright, refreshing aperitif that captures the essence of Mediterranean sunsets. The bitterness of the botanicals meets the effervescence of tonic, while a squeeze of orange adds just enough sweetness to round everything out.

Ice cubes

2 ounces (60 ml) Ghia Original Aperitif

2 to 4 ounces (60 to 120 ml) tonic water, elderflower tonic, or ginger beer

1 orange slice

Fill a glass with ice. Pour in the Ghia, then top with tonic water. Start with less—you can always add more. Squeeze the orange slice over the drink to release its juice, then drop it in as a garnish. Give the drink a gentle stir and serve immediately.

> **NOTE:** *While any tonic works well here, elderflower tonic adds an extra layer of floral complexity that pairs particularly well with Ghia's botanical notes. For a lighter version, substitute club soda for the tonic.*

MAKE IT YOUR OWN

- Add a sprig of rosemary or thyme.
- Replace the tonic with sparkling wine for special occasions.
- Float a few fresh raspberries on top.
- Add a dash of orange bitters for extra complexity.

GHIA-BOLO

SERVES 1 • **PREP TIME:** 2 MINUTES

The diabolo might be the first "mocktail" ever invented—just syrup and bubbles, mixed together to make French kids feel fancy. My version swaps in Ghia and uses just a touch of syrup—enough to make it craveable but not too sweet. It's a playful and refreshing drink you'll want to make all summer long.

Ice cubes

2 ounces (60 ml) Ghia Original Aperitif

Splash of grenadine or other syrup (about ¼ ounce / 7 ml)

4 to 5 ounces (120 to 150 ml) sparkling water

Fresh mint sprig, for garnish

Lemon twist (optional)

Fill a glass with ice cubes. Pour in the Ghia, followed by the grenadine. The goal is to complement Ghia's flavors, not overwhelm them. Top with the sparkling water and stir gently to combine. Garnish with the mint and a lemon twist (if using).

MAKE IT YOUR OWN

- For summer parties, freeze mint leaves in the ice cubes.
- Instead of grenadine, lavender, elderflower, or violet syrup all work really nicely too!

ACKNOWLEDGMENTS

Making a cookbook has always been a dream and there are so many people, in no order of importance, to thank for making this dream come true for me. Maman, Papa, Manon, and Pilou, with your voracious appetites. Our love for food flows from Mymo's kitchen through all of us, and every recipe in this book carries the memory of our table.

Michele Crim, my literary agent, who believed in this project and in me long before I believed in myself.

Cassie Jones and Nicole Braun: Thank you for understanding that this book needed to feel like home. Your editorial guidance helped make my "a little bit of this" recipes usable, but mostly you helped me find my voice on every page and supported my vision all the way. I am infinitely grateful for you. Many thanks to Rachel Meyers, Renata De Oliveira, Yeon Kim, Erin Merlo, Julie Paulauski, Anna Brower, and the entire team at Morrow. To Cristina Krumsick and the Isetta team, thank you for putting it in the hands of so many people.

Hugh Davison, you were the easiest and most generous partner to work with. You captured not just the food but the feeling of these meals. You're the best, and I owe you forever.

Ana Thompson, for jumping in to help and designing this cover, and for knowing what I wanted even when I couldn't explain it. You are not just the coolest and funniest, you are also one of the most talented people I know.

Olivier Leone, my visionary friend, thank you for expanding your range from fashion campaigns to my grandfather's roast beef. You are an actual. Julia Zagury and Emma, your styling made every dish look like it belonged at my grandmother's table. I learned so much watching you work, and I now keep kitchen tweezers by my side at all times.

Leslie Kirchhoff, for developing drinks I wish I could bottle. I've never felt more at home in L.A. than in *the garden*, drinking your magical punches.

Laszlo Badet, I'm so happy you answered my DM and our collaboration and friendship bloomed through this process. Sarah Ehrmann, for the intense and meticulous work on our shoot. You were on your feet for so many goddamn hours—thank you.

To our recipe testers, Hannah Melde Webster, Chloe Walsh, Natacha Stojanovic, and Cathryn Greenwald, for your meticulous notes. You understood that I wanted these recipes to stay easy and adaptable, and let me borrow your fresh eyes when I was a bit cooked myself.

To Hôtel du Couvent and Tuba Club, thank you for opening your beautiful spaces to us. Few places capture the magic of the Riviera like your hotels and kitchens. And to Christofle and La Romaine Éditions, you made simple food look grand. My grandmother would call this "mettre les petits plats dans les grands."

To Gucci and CO, thank you for the last-minute suitcase of wonders. I still can't believe I wore these clothes in the kitchen.

To my fellow founder friends, especially Camilla, Jing, and Becca, watching you write your own cookbooks gave me permission to believe in mine. You're my real-life superheroes.

To the entire Ghia team, you brought my proposal to life and cheered me on through every late night of writing, and every morning I showed up late to the office because I'd gotten lost in these words.

And, finally, to Adam, my favorite person to cook with, my greatest cheerleader. I love you like you love tomatoes and the sea.

UNIVERSAL CONVERSION CHART

OVEN TEMPERATURE EQUIVALENTS

250°F = 120°C

275°F = 135°C

300°F = 150°C

325°F = 160°C

350°F = 180°C

375°F = 190°C

400°F = 200°C

425°F = 220°C

450°F = 230°C

475°F = 240°C

500°F = 260°C

MEASUREMENT EQUIVALENTS

Measurements should always be level unless directed otherwise.

⅛ teaspoon = 0.5 mL

¼ teaspoon = 1 mL

½ teaspoon = 2 mL

1 teaspoon = 5 mL

1 tablespoon = 3 teaspoons =
½ fluid ounce = 15 mL

2 tablespoons = ⅛ cup =
1 fluid ounce = 30 mL

4 tablespoons = ¼ cup =
2 fluid ounces = 60 mL

5⅓ tablespoons = ⅓ cup =
3 fluid ounces = 80 mL

8 tablespoons = ½ cup =
4 fluid ounces = 120 mL

10⅔ tablespoons = ⅔ cup =
5 fluid ounces = 160 mL

12 tablespoons = ¾ cup =
6 fluid ounces = 180 mL

16 tablespoons = 1 cup =
8 fluid ounces = 240 mL

INDEX

NOTE: Page references in *italics* indicate photographs.

hc.com

FIRST EDITION

DESIGN BY RENATA DE OLIVEIRA

Photographs by Hugh Davison
Additional photography by Alex Paganelli

Library of Congress Cataloging-in-Publication Data has been applied for.

ISBN 978-0-06-344575-8

26 27 28 29 30 TC 10 9 8 7 6 5 4 3 2 1